Elasticsearch 7 Quick Start Guide

Get up and running with the distributed search and analytics capabilities of Elasticsearch

Anurag Srivastava
Douglas Miller

BIRMINGHAM - MUMBAI

Elasticsearch 7 Quick Start Guide

Commissioning Editor: Amey Varangaonkar
Acquisition Editor: Reshma Raman
Content Development Editor: Roshan Kumar
Senior Editor: Jack Cummings
Technical Editor: Manikandan Kurup
Copy Editor: Safis Editing
Project Coordinator: Kirti Pisat
Proofreader: Safis Editing
Indexer: Tejal Daruwale Soni
Production Designer: Shraddha Falebhai

First published: October 2019

Production reference: 1231019

Published by Packt Publishing Ltd.
Livery Place
35 Livery Street
Birmingham
B3 2PB, UK.

ISBN 978-1-78980-332-7

www.packt.com

Packt>

Contributors

About the authors

Anurag Srivastava is a senior technical lead in a multinational software company. He has more than 12 years' experience in web-based application development. He is proficient in designing architecture for scalable and highly available applications. He has handled development teams and multiple clients from all over the globe over the past 10 years of his professional career. He has significant experience with the Elastic Stack (Elasticsearch, Logstash, and Kibana) for creating dashboards using system metrics data, log data, application data, and relational databases. He has authored three other books—*Mastering Kibana 6.x*, and *Kibana 7 Quick Start Guide*, and *Learning Kibana 7 - Second Edition*, all published by Packt.

Douglas Miller is an expert in helping fast-growing companies to improve performance and stability, and in building search platforms using Elasticsearch. Clients (including Walgreens, Nike, Boeing, and Dish Networks) have seen sales increase, fast performance times, and lower overall costs in terms of the total costs of ownership for their Elasticsearch clusters.

About the reviewer

Craig Brown is an independent consultant, offering services for Elasticsearch and other big data software. He is a core Java developer with 25+ years' experience and more than 10 years of Elasticsearch experience. He has also practiced with machine learning, Hadoop, and Apache Spark, is a co-founder of the Big Mountain Data user group in Utah, and is a speaker on Elasticsearch and other big data topics.

Craig has founded NosqlRevolution LLC, focusing on Elasticsearch and big data services, and PicoCluster LLC, a desktop data center designed for learning and prototyping cluster computing and big data frameworks.

Packt is searching for authors like you

If you're interested in becoming an author for Packt, please visit authors.packtpub.com and apply today. We have worked with thousands of developers and tech professionals, just like you, to help them share their insight with the global tech community. You can make a general application, apply for a specific hot topic that we are recruiting an author for, or submit your own idea.

Table of Contents

Preface

Elasticsearch is one of the most popular tools for distributed open source search and analytics. This book will help you in understanding everything about the new features of Elasticsearch, and how to use them efficiently for searching, aggregating, and indexing data with speed and accuracy, while also helping you understand how you can use them to build your own search applications with ease. You will also acquire a basic understanding of how to build and deploy effective search and analytics solutions using Elasticsearch.

Starting with an introduction to the Elastic Stack, this book will help you quickly get up to speed with using Elasticsearch. Next, you'll learn how to deploy and manage Elasticsearch clusters, as well as how to use your deployment to develop powerful search and analytics solutions. As you progress, you'll also discover how to install, configure, manage, and secure Elasticsearch clusters, in addition to understanding how to troubleshoot any issues you may encounter along the way. Finally, the book helps you explore the inner workings of Elasticsearch and gain insights into queries, analyzers, mappings, and aggregations as you learn to work with search results.

Who this book is for

This book is for software developers, engineers, data architects, system administrators, or anyone who wants to get up and running with Elasticsearch 7.

What this book covers

Chapter 1, *Introduction to Elastic Stack*, will give you a brief history and background on Elasticsearch. We will also get introduced to log analysis and will cover some of the core components of the Elastic Stack architecture.

Chapter 2, *Installing Elasticsearch*, will cover the installation process of Elasticsearch in different environments. We will also look into installation using the Debian and rpm packages, followed by installation on Windows using the MSI installer of Elasticsearch.

Chapter 3, *Many as One – the Distributed Model*, will cover how to interact with Elasticsearch using REST calls to call different operations. We will also look at how we can handle multiple indices, followed by looking at some of the common options for the API response. We will also learn how to create, delete, and retrieve indices.

Chapter 4, *Prepping Your Data – Text Analysis and Mapping,* will walk through the details of how full text is analyzed and indexed in Elasticsearch, followed by looking into some of the various analyzers and filters and how they can be configured. We will also learn how Elasticsearch mappings are used for defining documents and fields and storing and indexing them, including how to define multi-fields and custom analyzers.

Chapter 5, *Let's Do a Search!,* will go into further detail regarding data searches, where we will cover URI search and body search. We will also cover some query examples using term, from/size, sort, and source filtering. Following that, we will also cover highlighting, rescoring, search type, and named queries.

Chapter 6, *Performance Tuning,* will cover data sparsity and how to improve the performance of Elasticsearch. We will also cover how to adjust the search speed by means of allocating memory to the filesystem cache, faster hardware, document modeling, pre-index data, avoiding replicas, and so on.

Chapter 7, *Aggregating Datasets,* will cover how to aggregate datasets and will explain the different types of aggregations that Elasticsearch supports.

Chapter 8, *Best Practices,* will cover the best practices we can follow in order to manage an Elasticsearch cluster.

To get the most out of this book

No prior experience with the Elastic Stack is required. The steps for installing and running Elasticsearch are covered in the book.

Download the example code files

You can download the example code files for this book from your account at www.packt.com. If you purchased this book elsewhere, you can visit www.packtpub.com/support and register to have the files emailed directly to you.

You can download the code files by following these steps:

1. Log in or register at www.packt.com.
2. Select the **Support** tab.
3. Click on **Code Downloads**.
4. Enter the name of the book in the **Search** box and follow the onscreen instructions.

Once the file is downloaded, please make sure that you unzip or extract the folder using the latest version of:

- WinRAR/7-Zip for Windows
- Zipeg/iZip/UnRarX for Mac
- 7-Zip/PeaZip for Linux

The code bundle for the book is also hosted on GitHub at `https://github.com/PacktPublishing/Elasticsearch-7-Quick-Start-Guide`. In case there's an update to the code, it will be updated on the existing GitHub repository.

We also have other code bundles from our rich catalog of books and videos available at `https://github.com/PacktPublishing/`. Check them out!

Download the color images

We also provide a PDF file that has color images of the screenshots/diagrams used in this book. You can download it here: `http://www.packtpub.com/sites/default/files/downloads/9781789803327_ColorImages.pdf`.

Conventions used

There are a number of text conventions used throughout this book.

`CodeInText`: Indicates code words in text, database table names, folder names, filenames, file extensions, pathnames, dummy URLs, user input, and Twitter handles. Here is an example: "Let's take the example of `kibana_sample_data_flight` data to understand how we can prettify the results using the `pretty` keyword."

A block of code is set as follows:

```
PUT index_name
{
    "settings": {
        "number_of_shards": 1
    },
    "mappings": {
        "_doc": {
            "properties": {
                "field_number_1": {
                    "type": "text"
                }
            }
```

```
        }
      }
    }
```

Any command-line input or output is written as follows:

```
curl -L -O
https://artifacts.elastic.co/downloads/elasticsearch/elasticsearch-
7.1.1-linux-x86_64.tar.gz
```

Bold: Indicates a new term, an important word, or words that you see on screen. For example, words in menus or dialog boxes appear in the text like this. Here is an example: "A manual uninstall must be performed through **Add or remove programs**."

Warnings or important notes appear like this.

Tips and tricks appear like this.

Get in touch

Feedback from our readers is always welcome.

General feedback: If you have questions about any aspect of this book, mention the book title in the subject of your message and email us at customercare@packtpub.com.

Errata: Although we have taken every care to ensure the accuracy of our content, mistakes do happen. If you have found a mistake in this book, we would be grateful if you would report this to us. Please visit www.packtpub.com/support/errata, selecting your book, clicking on the Errata Submission Form link, and entering the details.

Piracy: If you come across any illegal copies of our works in any form on the internet, we would be grateful if you would provide us with the location address or website name. Please contact us at copyright@packt.com with a link to the material.

If you are interested in becoming an author: If there is a topic that you have expertise in, and you are interested in either writing or contributing to a book, please visit authors.packtpub.com.

Reviews

Please leave a review. Once you have read and used this book, why not leave a review on the site that you purchased it from? Potential readers can then see and use your unbiased opinion to make purchase decisions, we at Packt can understand what you think about our products, and our authors can see your feedback on their book. Thank you!

For more information about Packt, please visit `packt.com`.

Introduction to Elastic Stack 1

The Elastic Stack consists of Elasticsearch, Logstash, and Kibana, which together form the ELK Stack. Elasticsearch is an open source search engine developed by Shay Banon, with an easy-to-use web interface that provides excellent flexibility through plugins that expand the functionality of a wide range of applications. Because it is open source, it is easily accessible to everyone, and user input provides great feedback for ongoing, constant improvement of the product. Elasticsearch can be used for everything from simple to complex searches. For example, a simple search for old maps could involve counting the number of cartographers, or studying cartographers' products, or analyzing map contents. Many criteria can be used for searches, for a wide range of purposes.

Elasticsearch supports multi-tenancy, meaning it can store multiple indices on a server, and information can be retrieved from multiple indices using a single query. It uses documents with JSON format; for requests, responses, and during transfer, they are automatically indexed. In this chapter, we are going to cover the following topics:

- Brief history and background
- Why use Elasticsearch?
- What is log analysis?
- Elastic Stack architecture
- Use cases of the Elastic Stack

Brief history and background

Developed in 2012, Elastic is an open source company that develops a distributed open source search engine based on Lucene. The history of Elastic starts with its main founder, Shay Banon, who wanted to explore making searching easier. In 2004, he released his first open source search-based product called **Compass**. This first iteration of open source search tools served as an inspiration, and, from Compass onward, searching has improved.

Around Elasticsearch grew a small community that would later lead to important partnerships that grew the company's capabilities. Jordan Sissel was working on a plugin ingestion tool named Logstash that sent the user logs to a stash, and Elasticsearch was one of those stashes. A visualization engine was needed and was provided by Rashid Khan, who was working on Kibana. Other contributors provided their own features and add-ons, and, hence, a stack of software was developed. The main product of Elastic continues to be Elasticsearch, and this is the focus of the following chapters.

Why use Elasticsearch?

Elasticsearch can be used for analytics through the aggregations generated by Kibana. This uses both CPU and memory and can be rather expensive. When Elasticsearch needs to search documents for certain criteria, all of the data from all of the documents is loaded into a cache named field data. Doc values is a feature that allows users to store field values in a column, thus making it more practical for sorting and searching. This particular feature has its benefits—for example, it handles memory better and it updates the indexing times more rapidly—but this also leads to bigger indices. In turn, this problem can be solved by changing the field value to apply one criteria only. In this way, each potential problem with using Elasticsearch can be circumvented by features and plugins, making it an extremely versatile tool. Let's now move onto a process that helps in effectively managing applications and identifying any upcoming potential threat.

What is log analysis?

Log analysis is a process that we use to fetch and collect different types of log and then use tools to process them so that we can get information out of them. The advantages of log analysis include reducing problem diagnosis time, effective management of applications, and the identification of potential threats. Logs provide information about the operating system, network equipment, and devices, and they can be stored on a disk or in an application. For most companies, log analysis is an integral part of a security policy that helps them achieve certification.

The combination of Elasticsearch, Logstash, Kibana, and Beats is used for log search and analysis. It provides real-time data information about the online activity of users, and manages and analyzes this data. This is important for many businesses, organizations, and networks as it helps them understand user behavior, allows them to respond proactively, provides information about data breaches, and conducts forensics for investigations. Since indexing is document-oriented, it is able to work with large amounts of data. Logstash and Beats aggregate the logs and process them, after which the data is then sent to Elasticsearch for indexing. Elasticsearch indexes different logs and stores them, and Kibana can fetch those logs to analyze or visualize them by creating dashboards.

Elastic Stack architecture

As mentioned previously, the Elastic Stack consists of four components—Elasticsearch, Kibana, Logstash, and Beats. To understand the architecture of the stash, let's look in more detail at some important terms. Please refer to the following diagram to learn more about these components:

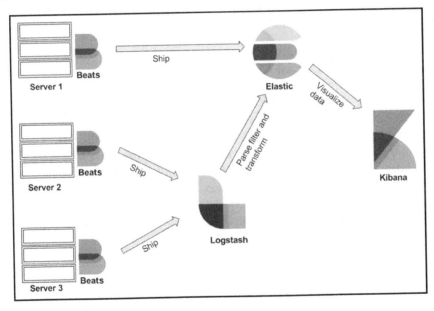

As you can see, in Elastic Stack, Beats and Logstash send data to Elasticsearch, where the data is stored. Kibana is the UI of Elastic Stack; it reads the Elasticsearch data to create graphical charts and more. Now, let's cover each of the components in detail, so let's start with Elasticsearch.

Elasticsearch

Elasticsearch provides the searching and management functionality of a document-oriented database. Documents are stored in JSON form, and, with the help of a query DSL, any document can be retrieved. It uses an HTTP interface, and REST APIs are used to index, search, retrieve, delete, or update the database. Elasticsearch is used by so many because it allows the user to write a single query that can perform complex searches (such as by applying certain conditions). Elasticsearch has three main uses: web search, log analysis, and big data analytics. It is widely used by big companies such as Netflix, Stack Overflow, and Accenture (among others) to monitor performance, analyze user operations, and keep track of security logs.

A relational database system is a cluster of databases in which each database is called an index. The tables in the index are named type, each row is a document, and each column is a field. The process of defining how a document and its fields are stored and indexed is called mapping. A query DSL is a SQL query that requests information from a database. A cluster is a collection of servers that contain the entirety of the data. The default name for the cluster is Elasticsearch. Each cluster is made up of nodes, which are the individual servers. They store the data and are indexed to the cluster. A collection of documents that contain similar characteristics is called an index. There is no limit on how many indices there can be in a cluster.

The information that can be indexed is called a document. It is expressed in JSON format, and it can store various pieces of data. Shards are subdivisions of an index and can help in cases of strict hardware limits, or when the lag time increases due to large amounts of data. Shards split data horizontally and are considered to be indices themselves. Distribution and even parallel operations can be performed on multiple shards. Replicas are copies of a shard or a node in case of failures. They are allocated to a different node and allow scalability because searches can be performed in parallel on all replicas. The features of Elasticsearch are based on REST APIs. The Index API is used to add a JSON form document to an index and make it accessible for searches. The Get API is used to retrieve those documents from their index, while the Delete API removes the document entirely. The Update API updates the document according to a script.

Kibana

Kibana is an open source interactive visualization and analytics plugin used by Elastic. It offers the user different ways to represent their data: charts, tables, maps, dashboards, and so on. It also lets the user perform searches and visualize and interact with data to perform advanced analysis.

Kibana uses a browser-based interface that is incredibly easy to use, and it displays real-time Elasticsearch queries. It has a machine learning feature that models the behavior of the data, learning trends, and more so that anomalies are detected as soon as possible.

Logstash

Logstash is an open source pipeline that collects data from multiple sources, processes them, and forwards events and log messages along with the data to a stash—in this case, to Elasticsearch. Its architecture makes it easy to mix and match various inputs, filters, and outputs. As with Elasticsearch, Logstash allows users to add plugins and contribute, creating flexibility. It transforms data into JSON documents, which are then delivered to Elasticsearch. But as well as a pipeline, it can be used for analysis, archiving, monitoring, and alerting.

The operating procedure starts with an input plugin that collects the data, which is then processed using filters that modify and annotate the event data. There are multiple pipelines that Logstash uses based on the configuration files. The user can specify single or multiple configuration files to create a single pipeline. The use of multiple pipelines is perfect for different logical flows, as it reduces the conditions and complexity of one pipeline. This configuration also offers easier maintenance.

An input plugin is a component that allows a specified source of events to be accessed by Logstash. A filter plugin then processes the event data, and this is often dependent on the characteristics of the event. An output plugin then sends the data to the destination specified. Plugin management is a script that manages the plugins by installation, listing, or removal.

Beats

Beats are basically lightweight data shippers that are designed for a very specific purpose. They can be installed on a standalone server, from where they fetch data or metrics and send them to Elasticsearch or Logstash. There are many types of Beats that we can use as needed; for example, if we want to process log file data, then we can use Filebeat, Packetbeat can be used to fetch network data, and Winlogbeat can be used if we want to fetch Windows events logs. Beats not only send data from a server, but also provides built-in dashboards and visualizations that we can easily configure in Kibana. Let's now discuss some of the important Elastic Beats.

Filebeat

Filebeat is a lightweight data shipper that can be installed on different servers to read file data. Filebeat monitors the log files that we specify in the configuration, collects the data from there in an incremental way, and then forwards them to Logstash or directly into Elasticsearch for indexing. After configuring Filebeat, it starts the input as per the given instructions. Filebeat starts a harvester to read a single log to get the incremental data for each separate file. Harvester sends the log data to libbeat, and then libbeat aggregates all events and sends the data to the output as per the given instructions, such as in Elasticsearch, Kafka, or Logstash. This way, we can configure Filebeat on any server to read the file data and send it to Elasticsearch for further analysis.

Metricbeat

Metricbeat is again a lightweight data shipper that can be installed on any server to fetch system metrics. Metricbeat helps us to collect metrics from systems and services with which we can monitor the servers. It fetches the metrics from the servers where they are installed and running. Metricbeat ships the collected system metrics data to Elasticsearch or Logstash for analysis. Metricbeat can monitor many different services; some of these are as follows:

- MySQL
- PostgreSQL
- Apache
- NGINX
- Redis
- HAProxy

Here, I have listed only some of the services, but Metricbeat supports a lot more than that.

Packetbeat

Using Packetbeat, we can analyze network packets in real time. Packetbeat data can be pushed into Elasticsearch, where it can be stored. We can configure Kibana to use the Metricbeat data from Elasticsearch for real-time application monitoring. Packetbeat is very effective at diagnosing network-related issues because it captures the network traffic between our application servers and it decodes the application layer protocols, such as HTTP, Redis, and MySQL. Packetbeat supports many different protocols; some of these are as follows:

- HTTP
- MySQL
- PostgreSQL
- Redis
- MongoDB
- Memcache
- TLS
- DNS

We can configure Packetbeat to send our network packet data directly to Elasticsearch or to Logstash. We just need to install and configure it on the server where you want to monitor the network packets, and we can start getting the packet data into Elasticsearch. Once Elasticsearch starts getting Packetbeat data, we can create a packet data monitoring dashboard using Kibana. Packetbeat also provides a custom dashboard that we can easily configure using the Packetbeat configuration file.

Auditbeat

We can install and configure Auditbeat on any server to audit the activities of users and processes. Auditbeat is a lightweight data shipper that sends the data directly to Elasticsearch or Logstash. Sometimes, it is difficult to track changes in binaries or configuration files because we never maintain the audit trail for the same. Auditbeat is helpful here because it detects changes to critical files, such as different configuration files and binaries. Auditbeat can help us to take that data and push it to Elasticsearch, from where Kibana can be configured to create dashboards.

Winlogbeat

Winlogbeat is a data shipper that we can use to ship Windows event logs to Logstash or the Elasticsearch cluster. It keeps a watch on Windows machines, reads from different Windows event logs, and sends them to Logstash or Elasticsearch in a timely manner. Winlogbeat can send different types of events, as follows:

- Hardware events
- Security events
- System events
- Application events

Winlogbeat sends structured data to Logstash or Elasticsearch after reading raw event data, which makes it easier to apply filter and aggregation on the data.

Heartbeat

Heartbeat is another lightweight data shipper that we can use to monitor a server's uptime. We can install Heartbeat on a remote server on which it periodically checks the status of different services and tells us whether they are available. The major difference between Metricbeat and Heartbeat is that Metricbeat tells us whether that server is up or down, while Heartbeat tells us whether services are reachable. Heartbeat is quite similar to the ping command, which tells us whether the server is responding.

Use cases of the Elastic Stack

The Elastic Stack can have multiple use cases, and we can use it in many areas, such as logging, data searching, and dashboarding; but these are just a few use cases of the Elastic Stack that we primarily use. There are many other areas where we can use the power of Elastic Stack. We can use the Elastic Stack for the following use cases.

System monitoring

We need to make our application stable by avoiding anything that can impact its performance. Anything that can hamper application performance, such as the system, database, or any third-party dependency. If anything fails, it will impact the application's performance. System monitoring using Elastic Stack can help us to avoid such situations where the system can impact application performance. There may be a number of reasons, such as if system memory or CPU is creating a bottleneck because of an increase in user hits. Using monitoring, we can configure the alert whenever the threshold value of any component increases. In this way, you can protect yourself from any application outage because of system performance.

Log management

Log management is one of the key use cases of Elastic Stack, and we have been using Elastic Stack for this purpose for many years. There are many benefits of log management using Elastic Stack. Let's say you have a log file and you need to explore it to get to the root cause of any issue in the application. So how are you going to proceed? One way is to open the log file in a text editor or terminal and search the issue. Another way is to push the log data into Elasticsearch and configure Kibana to read this data. We can use Filebeat to read the log files, such as Apache access and error logs. Apart from system logs, we can also configure Filebeat to capture application logs. This way, using Filebeat or Logstash, we can push the logs into Elasticsearch and can analyze that using Kibana.

Application performance monitoring

Using Elastic Stack APM, we can monitor applications for performance and availability. APM helps us to identify any current application issues or ones that may occur in the near future. We can find and fix any bug in the code using APM, as this makes the problems in the code searchable. By configuring APM with our application, we can monitor the code and make it better and more efficient. Elastic APM also provides us with custom preconfigured dashboards in Kibana that we can easily load. We can apply machine learning to APM data using the APM UI to find any anomaly in the data. We can also configure the alerts so that we can get the email notification if anything goes wrong in the code. Currently, Elastic APM supports Node.js, Python, Java, Ruby, Go, and JavaScript. It's easy to configure APM with the application, and it requires only a few lines of code to configure.

Data visualization

Data visualization is the main feature of Kibana, and using Kibana, we can create different types of charts, graphs, and so on. Kibana is popular because it has the capability to create dashboards for KPIs using data from different sources. We can push any structured and unstructured data into Elasticsearch, using Logstash or Beats. Once the data is in Elasticsearch, we can create visualizations by creating index patterns in Kibana for those indexes in Elasticsearch.

Summary

In this chapter, we introduced different aspects of Elastic Stack, starting with a brief history and background of Elasticsearch. Then, we explained why we use Elasticsearch, followed by log analysis. After an introduction to Elasticsearch, we covered other components under Elastic Stack architecture. Finally, we covered different use cases of Elastic Stack. In the next chapter, we will cover the installation process of Elasticsearch in different environments.

2
Installing Elasticsearch

In the last chapter, we introduced the Elastic Stack. We covered the basics and different use cases. Now we will focus on Elasticsearch and learn more about it. In this chapter, we will cover the Elasticsearch installation process on different operating systems. Elasticsearch can be installed and run on a computer or on the Elastic Cloud (assuming it's the hosted Elasticsearch service). The latter option uses **Amazon Web Services (AWS)** and **Google Cloud Platform (GCP)** to host Elasticsearch and Kibana, and users should note that to run the Elastic Stack, Java 8 or newer is needed. So, let's start the Elasticsearch installation process to understand how it can be installed on different operating systems. In this chapter, we are going to cover the following:

- Installing Elasticsearch on Linux or macOS
- Installing Elasticsearch using the Debian package
- Installing Elasticsearch using the `rpm` package
- Installing Elasticsearch using MSI Windows Installer
- Installing Elasticsearch on macOS

Installation of Elasticsearch

We will cover the different ways of installing Elasticsearch depending on the operating system we are using. Elasticsearch is the heart of the Elastic Stack, and it is used to store data so that we can perform data analysis and visualization. So, let's start with Elasticsearch installation on Linux-based operating systems.

Installing Elasticsearch on Linux

Follow these steps to install Elasticsearch on Linux:

1. The first step is to download the Elasticsearch 7.1.1 Linux TAR file, which we can do using the following command:

```
curl -L -O
https://artifacts.elastic.co/downloads/elasticsearch/elasticsearch-
7.1.1-linux-x86_64.tar.gz
```

2. After downloading the Linux TAR file, we need to extract it using the following command:

```
tar -xvf elasticsearch-7.1.1-linux-x86_64.tar.gz
```

3. It will then create a lot of files and folders in the current directory of Elasticsearch. We then go into the `bin` directory as follows:

```
cd elasticsearch-7.1.1/bin
```

4. And now we are ready to start our node and a single cluster using the following command:

```
./elasticsearch
```

Installing Elasticsearch using the Debian package

Follow these steps to install Elasticsearch using the Debian package:

1. First, install the `apt-transport-https` package using the following command:

```
sudo apt-get install apt-transport-https
```

2. Save the repository definition in `/etc/apt/sources.list.d/elastic-7.x.list`:

```
echo "deb https://artifacts.elastic.co/packages/7.x/apt stable
main" | sudo tee -a /etc/apt/sources.list.d/elastic-7.x.list
```

3. To install the Elasticsearch Debian package, run the following command:

```
sudo apt-get update && sudo apt-get install elasticsearch
```

That's how to install Elasticsearch using the Debian package.

Installing Elasticsearch using the rpm package

We need to do the following to install Elasticsearch using the rpm package:

1. Download and then install the public signing key:

```
rpm --import https://artifacts.elastic.co/GPG-KEY-elasticsearch
```

2. Create a file called elasticsearch.repo for RedHat-based distributions in the /etc/yum.repos.d/ directory. For openSUSE-based distributions, we have to create the file in the /etc/zypp/repos.d/ directory. We need to add the following entry to the file:

```
[elasticsearch-7.x]
name=Elasticsearch repository for 7.x packages
baseurl=https://artifacts.elastic.co/packages/7.x/yum
gpgcheck=1
gpgkey=https://artifacts.elastic.co/GPG-KEY-elasticsearch
enabled=1
autorefresh=1
type=rpm-md
```

After adding the preceding code, we can install Elasticsearch in a variety of environments.

3. We can run the yum command on **CentOS** and older versions of **RedHat**-based distributions:

```
sudo yum install elasticsearch
```

4. On Fedora and other newer versions of RedHat distributions, use the dnf command:

```
sudo dnf install elasticsearch
```

5. The `zypper` command can be used on **openSUSE**-based distributions:

```
sudo zypper install elasticsearch
```

6. The Elasticsearch service can be started or stopped using the following command:

```
sudo -i  service elasticsearch start
sudo -i  service elasticsearch stop
```

This way we can install Elasticsearch using the `rpm` package.

Installing rpm manually

Install the `rpm` package manually using the following steps.

1. We can download the `rpm` package for Elasticsearch v7.1.1 from the website using the following command:

```
wget
https://artifacts.elastic.co/downloads/elasticsearch/elasticsearch-
7.1.1-x86_64.rpm
```

2. After downloading the `rpm` package we can compare the SHA of the downloaded `rpm` using the following command:

```
wget
https://artifacts.elastic.co/downloads/elasticsearch/elasticsearch-
7.1.1-x86_64.rpm.sha512
shasum -a 512 -c elasticsearch-7.1.1-x86_64.rpm.sha512
```

3. Once the `rpm` package is downloaded, we can install it using the following command:

```
sudo rpm --install elasticsearch-7.1.1-x86_64.rpm
```

This way we can install the `rpm` package manually. After installing Elasticsearch, we can run the service using two methods: SysV and systemd.

SysV

To run Elasticsearch using SysV, perform the following steps:

1. We can use the `chkconfig` command to configure Elasticsearch to start automatically every time the system boots up:

```
sudo chkconfig --add elasticsearch
```

2. We can start or stop Elasticsearch using the `service` command:

```
sudo -i service elasticsearch start
sudo -i service elasticsearch stop
```

systemd

To run Elasticsearch using systemd, perform the following steps:

1. We can configure Elasticsearch to start automatically every time the system boots up by running the following commands:

```
sudo /bin/systemctl daemon-reload
sudo /bin/systemctl enable elasticsearch.service
```

2. We can start or stop Elasticsearch using the following command:

```
sudo systemctl start elasticsearch.service
sudo systemctl stop elasticsearch.service
```

Installing Elasticsearch using MSI Windows Installer

Download the installation file from the MSI installation link. After the download is complete, double-click on the file and a GUI will open. I have installed 7.0.0-beta1, and that is why I am showing the steps using the following screenshots, but you can install the latest version, which is 7.4 at the time of writing this book. For the pre-released Elasticsearch 7.0.0, there will be a notification window asking users not to use pre-releases in production:

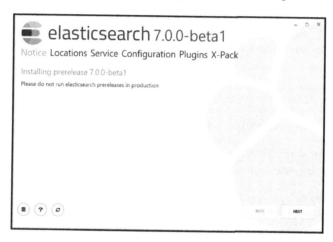

After clicking on the **NEXT** button, the first installation screen will show the directories that will be created during setup. This is the user's opportunity to manually alter the setup directories:

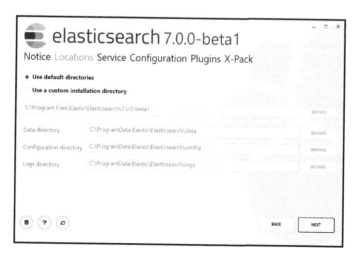

The next step requires the user to select the type of installation required. We can select it as a service or through manual installation, based on the requirement:

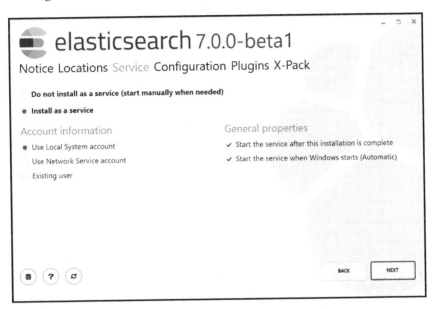

During configuration, we can see the default values that are used at each stage for simplicity. We can change these values, such as the name of the cluster or the memory allocation, as shown in the following screenshot:

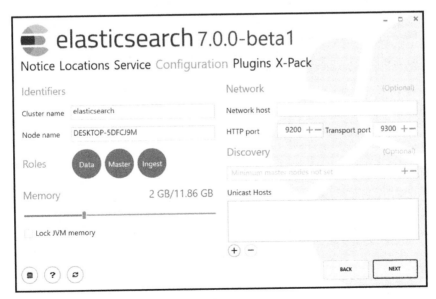

After tweaking the configurations we can click on the **NEXT** button, which will open the plugin view, from where we can pick and install the plugins. To install plugins, select the checkbox to select the plugins we want to install:

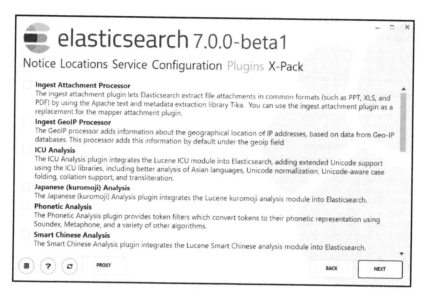

In the next step, we can select the type of license we want to use, such as basic or trial, by selecting it from the **License** dropdown. After selecting the license type, we need to click on the **INSTALL** button:

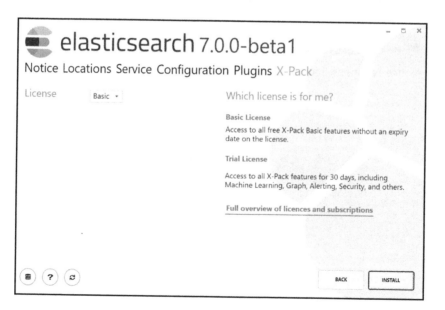

After clicking on the **INSTALL** button, the installation process will start, which we can see in the following screenshot:

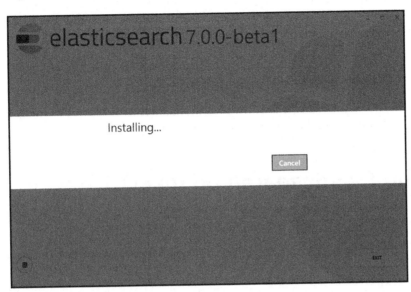

Once the installation process has been completed successfully, we will get a success message, as shown in the following screenshot:

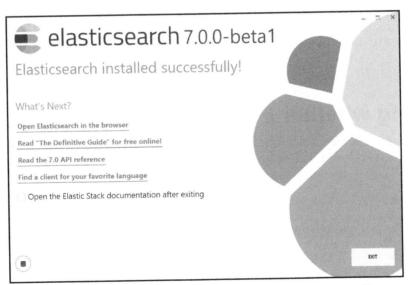

That's how to install Elasticsearch using MSI Windows Installer.

Elasticsearch upgrade on Windows

To upgrade using the GUI, download the new MSI file from the Elasticsearch website. Open the file and run the upgrade, following the prompts as with the preceding installation steps. The upgrade will retain the previous data and configurations.

Uninstall Elasticsearch on Windows

Elasticsearch does not provide an MSI file to uninstall the program. A manual uninstall must be performed through **Add or remove programs**.

Installing Elasticsearch on macOS

We can install Elasticsearch on macOS using the Homebrew package of Elasticsearch. We need to do the following to install Elasticsearch on macOS:

1. Tap on the Homebrew repository of Elasticsearch using the following command:

    ```
    brew tap elastic/tap
    ```

2. After tapping the Elastic Homebrew package we can install the default distribution of Elasticsearch using the `brew install` command:

    ```
    brew install elastic/tap/elasticsearch-full
    ```

Using the preceding command, we can install the most recent release of Elasticsearch on macOS.

Checking whether Elasticsearch is running

We can check whether Elasticsearch is running by sending an HTTP request on the Elasticsearch host and port. For example, if Elasticsearch is installed on the local machine, we can test by hitting the following command in the command line:

```
curl -X GET "localhost:9200/"
```

After hitting the preceding command, we get the following response if Elasticsearch is running:

```
{
  "name" : "KELLGGNLPTP0305",
  "cluster_name" : "elasticsearch",
```

```
  "cluster_uuid" : "BIP_9t5fR-SxB72hLM8SwA",
  "version" : {
    "number" : "7.1.1",
    "build_flavor" : "default",
    "build_type" : "deb",
    "build_hash" : "7a013de",
    "build_date" : "2019-05-23T14:04:00.380842Z",
    "build_snapshot" : false,
    "lucene_version" : "8.0.0",
    "minimum_wire_compatibility_version" : "6.8.0",
    "minimum_index_compatibility_version" : "6.0.0-beta1"
  },
  "tagline" : "You Know, for Search"
}
```

This way, we can verify that the Elasticsearch node is running. The output provides some additional details, such as the version number, build type, Lucene version, cluster name, and cluster UUID (short for **Universally Unique Identifier**).

Summary

In this chapter, we have covered the installation of Elasticsearch on different operating systems. We started with installation on Linux and macOS. Then we covered installation using the Debian and rpm packages. We also covered installing Elasticsearch manually using the rpm package. After that, we covered installation on Windows using the MSI installer of Elasticsearch. Then we covered how to install Elasticsearch on macOS using Homebrew. Finally, we covered how to check whether Elasticsearch is running by hitting the Elasticsearch URL. In this way, we have covered the process of installing Elasticsearch on different operating systems. In the next chapter, we will cover how to interact with Elasticsearch using REST calls to call different operations.

Many as One – the Distributed Model

3

Every single server of Elasticsearch is considered a node, and multiple nodes form a cluster. Elasticsearch uses clusters to provide scalability and redundancy. If a search is performed on a cluster, all of the nodes within it will be included in the search. For the most productive environment, it is best to use multiple nodes on different machines, with each one performing a specific task. A less efficient route is to use multiple nodes on the same machine—this is undoubtedly slower and is only really appropriate when testing high-availability features.–

Elasticsearch stores JSON documents and uses Lucene as a backend search engine. It indexes the documents, as well as their contents, so queries can be performed on fields as well. This makes searching very easy. Simple queries can be built using a field name or full text to search in a document. Elasticsearch performs more advanced searches as well, such as grouping queries together to get a more complex result. Additionally, value boosting is an available feature whereby the search prioritizes certain requirements.

Cluster APIs are cluster-level APIs that operate on a set of nodes (selected with node filters) in a specific cluster. These node filters are written in the form of JSON and contain conditions, such as adding and removing nodes from the set, according to the filter requirements. The filters include `_all`, `_local`, and `_master`, and the node ID or name can be used. The * symbol is a wildcard that can be used to retrieve a name or an address using partial information. In this chapter, we are going to cover the following topics:

- How to handle multiple indices
- Common options for the API response
- Cluster state and statistics
- Node state and statistics
- Index APIs
- Document APIs

API conventions

The Elasticsearch REST module allows Elasticsearch APIs to be exposed over HTTP using JSON. We can perform different operations on Elasticsearch using APIs, such as monitoring the cluster health, checking nodes, indices, and shards, or creating, updating, or deleting the index. So, ideally, we can do everything using the REST-based API, which we can use to interact with Elasticsearch. We will discuss these APIs in detail later in this chapter, but for now, let's learn how to handle multiple indices if we want to interact with them simultaneously.

Handling multiple indices

APIs can be applied to multiple indices using a list of indices, a wildcard index, or all of the indices, by using the `_all` notation. Elasticsearch supports the following URL query string parameters for all multi-index APIs:

- The `ignore_unavailable` phrase can be set to `true` or `false` to include or not include nonexistent indices or closed indices.
- The `allow_no_indices` phrase can be set to `true` or `false` to control whether the process will fail if a wildcard index expression leads to no indices.
- The `expand_wildcards` phrase can be set to open or closed to include open or closed indices.

We can also search over a range of time-series indices. This is called a date math index, and it takes the following form:

```
<static_name{date_math_expr{date_format|time_zone}}>
```

In the previous expression, `static_name` is the static part of the name, `date_math_expr` is the dynamic date math expression, `date_format` is the format of the date (this defaults to `YYYY.MM.DD.`), and `time_zone` is the time zone.

Instructions to execute the Elasticsearch queries:

To explain the queries in a cleaner way, we have not used the complete `curl` command which we can execute from the Terminal. All queries in this book can directly be executed in the Kibana DevTools Console, so I suggest you install Kibana to execute the Elasticsearch queries. But if you don't want to install Kibana, you can modify the queries in the following way:

Let's say you have the following query:

```
GET /_search
{
   "query": {
      "match_all": {}
   }
}
```

If you want to execute this query in the terminal with the CURL command, you can write the query in the following way:

```
curl -XGET "http://localhost:9200/_search" -d'
{
   "query": {
      "match_all": {}
   }
}'
```

This way, you can execute the same query in a terminal using a `curl` command.

Common options for the API response

We can hit the Elasticsearch APIs for getting the desired response, but if we want to modify the API response so that we change the display format or filter out some fields, then we can apply these options along with the query. There are some common options that can be applied to APIs, including the following:

- For pretty formatted results, append `?pretty=true` to any JSON request. This is recommended for debugging only. Let's take the example of `kibana_sample_data_flights` data to understand how we can prettify the results using the `pretty` keyword in the following expression:

  ```
  GET kibana_sample_data_flights/_search?pretty
  ```

  Using the previous expression, we can output the query result in a `pretty` format that is easy to understand because of the formatting, as you can see from the following result:

  ```
  {
    "took" : 0,
    "timed_out" : false,
    "_shards" : {
      "total" : 1,
      "successful" : 1,
      "skipped" : 0,
      "failed" : 0
    },
    "hits" : {
      "total" : {
        "value" : 10000,
        "relation" : "gte"
      },
      "max_score" : 1.0,
      "hits" : [
        {
          "_index" : "kibana_sample_data_flights",
          "_type" : "_doc",
          "_id" : "4Gg7g2sB9_x5jgks7lTj",
          "_score" : 1.0,
          "_source" : {
            "FlightNum" : "9HY9SWR",
            "DestCountry" : "AU",
            "OriginWeather" : "Sunny",
            "OriginCityName" : "Frankfurt am Main",
            "AvgTicketPrice" : 841.2656419677076,
            "DistanceMiles" : 10247.856675613455,
  ```

```
                    "FlightDelay" : false,
                    "DestWeather" : "Rain",
                    "Dest" : "Sydney Kingsford Smith International Airport",
                    "FlightDelayType" : "No Delay",
                    "OriginCountry" : "DE",
                    "dayOfWeek" : 0,
                    "DistanceKilometers" : 16492.32665375846,
                    "timestamp" : "2019-06-17T00:00:00",
                    "DestLocation" : {
                      "lat" : "-33.94609833",
                      "lon" : "151.177002"
                    },
                    "DestAirportID" : "SYD",
                    "Carrier" : "Kibana Airlines",
                    "Cancelled" : false,
                    "FlightTimeMin" : 1030.7704158599038,
                    "Origin" : "Frankfurt am Main Airport",
                    "OriginLocation" : {
                      "lat" : "50.033333",
                      "lon" : "8.570556"
                    },
                    "DestRegion" : "SE-BD",
                    "OriginAirportID" : "FRA",
                    "OriginRegion" : "DE-HE",
                    "DestCityName" : "Sydney",
                    "FlightTimeHour" : 17.179506930998397,
                    "FlightDelayMin" : 0
                }
            }
        }
```

The preceding JSON response is showing a single document of `kibana_sample_data_flights` data.

- By default, the results are returned in JSON format, which we can change into YAML format by providing `format=yaml` in the query, as shown in the following expression:

  ```
  GET kibana_sample_data_flights/_search?format=yaml
  ```

- There are some human-readable values that will return results in a way that is easier for us to understand. For example, 3,600,000 milliseconds is confusing, but 1 hour is clear. Set `human=true` to transform the result into a more readable response, as shown in the following expression:

  ```
  GET kibana_sample_data_flights/_search?human=true
  ```

- Using the `filter_path` parameter in a query, we can reduce the response from Elasticsearch. It supports a list of filters or the wildcard character to match a field name or partial field name. Let's take the example of `kibana_sample_data_flights` data to see how `filter_path` can help us to return selected fields only in the output. For example, if we only want to display the `FlightNum` and `Carrier` fields from the index, then we can write the expression in the following way:

```
GET
kibana_sample_data_flights/_search?filter_path=hits.hits._source.Fl
ightNum, hits.hits._source.Carrier
```

Using the previous expression, we can return the `FlightNum` and `Carrier` fields, as shown in the following result:

```
{
  "hits" : {
    "hits" : [
      {
        "_source" : {
          "FlightNum" : "9HY9SWR",
          "Carrier" : "Kibana Airlines"
        }
      },
      {
        "_source" : {
          "FlightNum" : "X98CCZO",
          "Carrier" : "Logstash Airways"
        }
      }
    ]}
}
```

- A `flat_settings` filter set to `true` will return the results in `flat` format. If set to `false`, it will return results in a more human-readable format:

```
GET kibana_sample_data_flights/_settings?flat_settings=true
```

Using the preceding expression, we can return the settings in a `flat` format; see the following result:

```
{
  "kibana_sample_data_flights" : {
    "settings" : {
      "index.auto_expand_replicas" : "0-1",
      "index.creation_date" : "1561274871175",
```

```
         "index.number_of_replicas" : "0",
         "index.number_of_shards" : "1",
         "index.provided_name" : "kibana_sample_data_flights",
         "index.uuid" : "BPB230Z0RdS3L2yJ-YTKJA",
         "index.version.created" : "7010199"
      }
   }
}
```

By default, `flat_settings` is set to `false`, so if we hit the `settings` endpoint without setting it to `true`, then we can get the result in the following format:

```
{
  "kibana_sample_data_flights" : {
    "settings" : {
      "index" : {
        "number_of_shards" : "1",
        "auto_expand_replicas" : "0-1",
        "provided_name" : "kibana_sample_data_flights",
        "creation_date" : "1561274871175",
        "number_of_replicas" : "0",
        "uuid" : "BPB230Z0RdS3L2yJ-YTKJA",
        "version" : {
          "created" : "7010199"
        }
      }
    }
  }
}
```

The preceding result shows the default output of the `settings` endpoint API where we can see the expanded view of the JSON code. APIs support a wide range of parameters—Boolean values, number values, time units, byte size units, distance units, as well as quantities with no units. They also enable stack traces in case of errors. Furthermore, Elasticsearch supports URL-based access control. Many users use proxies to access the indices, and this can lead to users inadvertently overriding indices. To prevent this, set `rest.action.multi.allow_explicit_index: false` to false in the `elasticsearch.yml` file.

Cluster state and statistics

Until now, we have seen different options that can be used to customize the output of Elasticsearch APIs. Now we will see how to manage the cluster, node, and more, using these APIs. So, let's start by looking at the cluster health status and statistics APIs.

Cluster health status

To retrieve cluster health status information, we need to run the following query through the _cluster endpoint:

```
GET _cluster/health
```

After executing the preceding query, we get the following response:

```
{
  "cluster_name" : "elasticsearch",
  "status" : "yellow",
  "timed_out" : false,
  "number_of_nodes" : 1,
  "number_of_data_nodes" : 1,
  "active_primary_shards" : 131,
  "active_shards" : 131,
  "relocating_shards" : 0,
  "initializing_shards" : 0,
  "unassigned_shards" : 1,
  "delayed_unassigned_shards" : 0,
  "number_of_pending_tasks" : 0,
  "number_of_in_flight_fetch" : 0,
  "task_max_waiting_in_queue_millis" : 0,
  "active_shards_percent_as_number" : 99.24242424242425
}
```

The preceding expression shows the cluster health output of Elasticsearch. Here, we can see the various details of the cluster, such as the name of the cluster, status, whether it has timed out, the number of nodes, the number of data nodes, the number of active primary shards, the number of active shards, the number of initializing shards, the number of pending tasks, and more.

A cluster's health indicates the health of the cluster, along with its capability and request success. For example, a cluster that indicates **yellow** health is functional, but is at risk of data loss as the nodes are either unassigned or all are assigned to the same node. For backup reasons, it's recommended that you use more than one node.

Cluster state

The cluster state retrieves information about the comprehensive state of the cluster. Using the following query, we can retrieve the cluster state:

```
GET _cluster/state
```

The cluster state query can be filtered using response filters, such as the following:

```
GET /_cluster/state/{metrics}/{indices}
```

In the preceding query, each filter depends on the number of shards and indices in the mapping. The metrics can be a list of metrics separated by commas, such as the following:

- The `version` phrase retrieves the version of the cluster state.
- The `master_node` phrase returns the elected master node part of the response.
- The `nodes` phrase returns the elected nodes part of the response.
- The `routing_table` phrase returns the routing table part of the response; a list of indices can be specified to return information pertaining to those indices.
- The `metadata` phrase returns the metadata part of the response; a list of indices can be added for a more specific search.
- The `blocks` phrase returns the block part of the response.

Cluster stats

The cluster stats APIs retrieve information from the overall cluster. They retrieve basic index metrics, such as memory usage, shard numbers, and information about the nodes in the cluster (including the number of nodes, the installed plugins, and the operating system). We can see the cluster statistics using the following command:

```
GET _cluster/stats
```

We can restrict the stats by applying the node filter using the following query:

```
GET /_cluster/stats/nodes/node_name_1, master:false
```

The preceding query will retrieve information about all the nodes except the first.

Cluster administration

A cluster can reroute the locations of shards to nodes. So if we want to explicitly move a shard from one node to another, then we can execute the `reroute` command, as shown in the following example:

```
POST /_cluster/reroute
{
    "commands": [{
            "move": {
                "index": "reroute_me","shard": 0,
                "from_node": "node1", "to_node": "node2"
            }
        },
        {
            "allocate_replica": {
                "index": "reroute_me","shard": 1,
                "node": "node3"
            }
        }
    ]
}
```

This will reroute the 0 shard with the `reroute_me` index from node 1 to node 2, and create a replica in node 3. The following commands are used:

- `move`: Moves the shard to another node; it selects the index name or shard number.
- `from_node`: Selects the location of the shard from the node number.
- `to_node`: Selects the location of the shard that will be transferred to the node number.
- `cancel`: Cancels the allocation of the shard.

Note that the cluster needs to maintain a balance, and Elasticsearch will reallocate to ensure this balance. The automatic reallocation can be turned off in the `cluster.routing.allocation.enable` settings.

The cluster settings can be reviewed with `GET /_cluster/settings`.

Updates can be set to `persistent` (meaning that they apply restarts) or `transient` (meaning that they do not survive a cluster restart), as shown in the following code:

```
PUT /_cluster/settings{
...
"persistent" : {...},
"transient" : {...}
}
```

The order of cluster precedence is as follows:

1. Transient cluster settings
2. Persistent cluster settings
3. Settings in the `elasticsearch.yml` configuration file

So, in this way, we can handle the cluster health, state, and statistics using different APIs. Now, let's continue and see how this can be done at the node level and how we can get the node state and statistics.

Node state and statistics

We have APIs to check the node details, and using those APIs we can fetch the desired details about any node. To retrieve information about the node, use the following commands:

```
GET /_nodes
GET /_nodes/_all
```

Using the preceding commands, we can get the details of the nodes. The second command selects all nodes that are to be run in the search. The following expression shows a snippet of the result that we can get after executing the second query:

```
{
    "_nodes": {
        "total": 1,
        "successful": 1,
        "failed": 0
    },
    "cluster_name": "elasticsearch",
    "nodes": {
        "OsuaWgbGQd2KXbWE3ENfEg": {
            "name": "KELLGGNLPTP0305",
            "transport_address": "127.0.0.1:9300",
            "host": "127.0.0.1",
            "ip": "127.0.0.1",
```

```
        "version": "7.1.1",
        "build_flavor": "default",
        "build_type": "deb",
        "build_hash": "7a013de",
        "total_indexing_buffer": 103887667,
        "roles": [
            "master",
            "data",
            "ingest"
        ]
    }
  }
}
```

The preceding expression shows the result of the GET /_nodes/_all query, in which we can see the node details. Using these commands, we can retrieve the following statistics about the nodes:

- The host phrase is the node's hostname.
- The IP phrase is the node's IP address.
- The name phrase is the node's name.
- The total_indexing_buffer phrase is the total heap that holds recently indexed documents before being written on the disk.
- The transport_address phrase is the host and port where HTTP connections are accepted.
- The version phrase is the version of Elasticsearch running on the node.

Apart from _all, we have some other flags that we can use, along with the GET /_nodes/ command, such as the following:

- The GET /_nodes/_local phrase selects the local node.
- The GET /_nodes/_master phrase selects the master node.
- The GET /_nodes/_name_* phrase selects the nodes with that name, or that include a wildcard.
- The GET /_nodes/_master:true or GET /_nodes/_master:false phrase can be used to select nodes according to their role.

Operating system information

To retrieve information about the operating system, simply add the os flag (for example, GET _nodes/os). The following expression shows the os block of the result:

```
"os" : {
        "refresh_interval_in_millis" : 1000,
        "name" : "Linux",
        "pretty_name" : "Ubuntu 19.04",
        "arch" : "amd64",
        "version" : "5.0.0-16-generic",
        "available_processors" : 4,
        "allocated_processors" : 4
    }
}
```

The preceding expression shows the os block of the result that we can get after executing the GET _nodes/os command. In this expression, we can get some important details about the os, such as the following:

- The os.name phrase retrieves information about the name of the operating system.
- The os.version phrase retrieves information about the version of the operating system.
- The os.available_processors phrase retrieves information about the number of processors available for the virtual machine.
- The os.allocated_processors phrase retrieves the number of processors that are actually being used in the thread pool size. This number can be set, but can never be larger than 32.

Process information

To retrieve the process information about the running processes, the process flag is used (for example, GET _nodes/process). Using this command, we can get the process details, as shown in the following expression:

```
"process" : {
        "refresh_interval_in_millis" : 1000,
        "id" : 2779,
        "mlockall" : false
    }
```

`process.id` retrieves the **process identifier (PID)**, and `process.refresh_interval_in_millis` retrieves the refresh interval.

Plugin information

To retrieve information about plugins and modules installed in the nodes, the following command is used:

```
GET /_nodes/plugins
```

Using the preceding command, we can get the details of plugins and modules. The following expression shows a snippet of the module:

```
"modules" : [
        {
          "name" : "aggs-matrix-stats",
          "version" : "7.1.1",
          "elasticsearch_version" : "7.1.1",
          "java_version" : "1.8",
          "description" : "Adds aggregations whose input are a list of
numeric fields and output includes a matrix.",
          "classname" :
"org.elasticsearch.search.aggregations.matrix.MatrixAggregationPlugin",
          "extended_plugins" : [ ],
          "has_native_controller" : false
        }]
```

The preceding expression shows the `aggs-matrix-stats` module details. The `GET /_nodes/plugins` phrase is similar to `os.available_processors` and retrieves the number of available processors in a node.

Index APIs

An index is a place where data is stored, and it points to one or more physical shards. As mentioned previously, a shard is a worker unit that stores a certain amount of data in the index. A shard is a division of the data in the index that distributes the data in the Elasticsearch cluster. Since Elasticsearch is dynamic, shards commute between nodes to ensure balance in the cluster. When creating an index, a set number of primary shards is fixed. A node can have as many shard replicas as needed, and there is no restriction.

We can create an index using the following command:

```
PUT index_name
{
    "Settings": {
        "number_of_shards": 4
        "number_of_replicas": 1
    }
}
```

The create index API also allows us to create the mapping. We can create the mapping using the following command:

```
PUT index_name
{
    "settings": {
        "number_of_shards": 1
    },
    "mappings": {
        "_doc": {
            "properties": {
                "field_number_1": {
                    "type": "text"
                }
            }
        }
    }
}
```

To delete an index, use the DELETE command followed by the index name to be deleted:

```
DELETE /index_name
```

To delete more indices, add a comma to separate the list:

```
DELETE /index_name1, index_name2, index_name3
```

Note that function _all or * can be used to delete all indices or only those with a wildcard.

Using the GET method, we can retrieve information about the indices, as shown in the following code:

```
GET /index_name
```

This way, we can create, delete, and get the index using the preceding APIs.

Document APIs

Using document APIs, we can create, list, and delete the documents in an index. Now, let's look at these APIs in detail, starting with single-document APIs first.

Single-document APIs

Single-document APIs are those APIs that we can use to play around with a single document—for example, we can create a new document, delete a document, and perform other actions. Now, let's discuss these operations in detail.

Creating a document

The index API is used to add or update a JSON document to a specific index. The following expression shows the command that we can use to create a document in the index:

```
PUT test_index/_doc/1
{
    "user": "user_name",
    "Post_date": "2001-01-01T10-10-10"
}
```

After executing the preceding command, we get the following output from the API:

```
{
  "_index" : "test_index",
  "_type" : "_doc",
  "_id" : "1",
  "_version" : 1,
  "result" : "created",
  "_shards" : {
    "total" : 2,
    "successful" : 1,
    "failed" : 0
  },
  "_seq_no" : 0,
  "_primary_term" : 1
}
```

In the preceding result, `total` indicates the number of shard copies, `failed` indicates the replication-related errors, and `successful` indicates the number of shards successfully copied.

The automatic indexing of documents is created with the `action.auto_create_index` setting. If set to `true`, it will automatically create indices; if set to `false`, it disables the automatic index creation:

```
PUT _cluster/settings
{
  "persistent":
  {
      "action.auto_create_index": "true"
  }
}
```

After executing the preceding command, we get the following result:

```
{
  "acknowledged" : true,
  "persistent" : {
    "action" : {
      "auto_create_index" : "true"
    }
  },
  "transient" : { }
}
```

Unless specified otherwise, when an index operation is executed, an ID is automatically generated. The POST phrase will be used instead of PUT and ID will be created.

Viewing a document

Using the get API (shown in the following code), we can retrieve a JSON-type document using the ID of the document:

```
GET test_index/_doc/1
```

The preceding command shows the GET method that we can use to retrieve the document with ID 1 from the index named test_index. After executing the command, we get the following result:

```
{
  "_index" : "test_index",
  "_type" : "_doc",
  "_id" : "1",
  "_version" : 1,
  "_seq_no" : 0,
  "_primary_term" : 1,
  "found" : true,
  "_source" : {
```

```
        "user" : "user_name",
        "Post_date" : "2001-01-01T10-10-10"
    }
}
```

This way, we can retrieve any document just by providing the ID of the document in the query.

We can provide additional parameters in the get API to tweak the results:

- The `realtime` parameter can be set to `true` or `false`, and it returns the values in real time.
- Using the `_source` parameter, we can return the selected fields instead of all fields of the document.

Deleting a document

The delete API (shown in the following code) allows the deletion of a document from a specific index, as shown in the following command:

```
DELETE test_index/_doc/1
```

The preceding command shows the `DELETE` method that we can use to delete the document with ID 1 from the index named `test_index`. After executing the command, we get the following result:

```
{
    "_index" : "test_index",
    "_type" : "_doc",
    "_id" : "1",
    "_version" : 2,
    "result" : "deleted",
    "_shards" : {
        "total" : 2,
        "successful" : 1,
        "failed" : 0
    },
    "_seq_no" : 1,
    "_primary_term" : 1
}
```

This way, we can delete any document by providing the document ID in the delete API.

Delete by query

Using the `_delete_by_query` API, we can delete documents that match with the provided query. This API is very useful as we can delete those documents that are returned using certain query conditions. The following expression shows the `_delete_by_query` command:

```
POST index_name/_delete_by_query
{
    "query": {
        "match": {}
    }
}
```

Here, `match` can be any parameter, such as date, number, or name. We get the following result after running the preceding command:

```
{
  "took" : 140,
  "timed_out": false,
  "deleted": 112,
  "batches": 1,
  "version_conflicts": 0,
  "noops": 0,
  "retries": {
    "bulk": 0,
    "search": 0
  },
  "throttled_millis": 0,
  "requests_per_second": -1.0,
  "throttled_until_millis": 0,
  "total": 119,
  "failures" : [ ]
}
```

This way, we can delete multiple documents based on the provided query expression.

Updating a document

To use the update API, use the `_update` parameter containing the required script changes. The parameters that can be used are `_index`, `_type`, `_id`, `_version`, `_routing`, and `_now`.

An update using a partial document will add the partial document fields to an existing document:

```
POST test_index/_doc/1/_update
{
  "doc": {
    "user": "anurag"
  }
}
```

We can update the document using the preceding command.

Multi-document APIs

Multi-document APIs are handled in a similar way to single-document APIs. Updating and deleting multi-documents uses the same parameters.

The multi-document API retrieves multiple documents using an index, type, or ID. Using `_mget` specifies the documents to be selected:

```
GET /test_index/_doc/_mget
{
    "ids" : ["1", "2"]
}
```

After executing the preceding command, we can list the documents with the IDs of 1 and 2.

The update by query API updates the documents in the index. The source is not changed:

```
POST node_name/_update_by_query
```

This takes a snapshot of the index as it starts, and will keep track of the changes to the document. It will return a conflict response if the document changes between the snapshot and the process of the request.

Summary

In this chapter, we covered the REST APIs that we can use to interact with Elasticsearch. We looked at how we can handle multiple indices and then moved on to look at the common options for the API response. We also covered the APIs for cluster health, state, and statistics to check the cluster details. After the cluster APIs, we covered the node APIs that we use to check the state and stats of the node. Then, we covered index APIs, learning how to create, delete, and retrieve indices. After looking at index APIs, we learned about document APIs and how we can use them to create, view, update, and delete documents, as well as using them to delete multiple documents using a query.

In the next chapter, we will walk through the details of how full text is analyzed and indexed in Elasticsearch, including a discussion of the various analyzers and filters and how to configure them. You will also learn how Elasticsearch mappings are used to define how your documents and fields are stored and indexed, including how to define multi-fields and custom analyzers.

4
Prepping Your Data – Text Analysis and Mapping

In the last chapter, we explained the distributed model of Elasticsearch and covered the different APIs that are supported in Elasticsearch. Here, we will discuss Elasticsearch analyzers and mapping, which is a very important aspect of data preparation as we need to tweak our data to get the relevant results through data search. Elasticsearch is very flexible for data analysis as it provides many built-in analyzers that we can pick, and we can even create our own analyzer.

Mapping can be dynamic or explicit; in dynamic mapping, Elasticsearch identifies the datatype for each field, which can be incorrect sometimes, while in explicit mapping, we create the mapping before indexing the actual data.

In this chapter, we are going to cover the following:

- What is an analyzer?
- Anatomy of an analyzer
- How to use an analyzer
- Normalizers
- Tokenizers
- Token filters
- Character filters

What is an analyzer?

Elasticsearch's analysis tool describes analysis as the process of converting text into tokens, which are then added to the inverted index and used for searching. Every analysis is performed by an analyzer. For example, an index time analysis built in English will convert a sentence into distinct words; these distinct words are the tokens. Take the example of the following sentence:

```
Hello World! This is my first program and these are my first lines.
```

This will be added to the inverted index as the following:

```
[hello, world, first, program, these, line]
```

The analyzer removes the most frequent words and reduces words to the word stem—so lines becomes line. An analyzer can be specified in the mapping in the text field, as shown in the following query:

```
PUT my_index
{
    "mappings": {
        "_doc": {
            "properties": {
                "title": {
                    "type": "text",
                    "analyzer": "standard"
                }
            }
        }
    }
}
```

If there is no index analyzer specified, it will default to standard. A similar process is performed on full-text queries. The text in the query string is changed into tokens similar to those stored in the inverted index, then it performs a search.

For example, if the search query is my first program, the query will be transformed into the following tokens:

```
[first, program]
```

The analyzer also changes uppercase characters into lowercase characters to ensure that the query will match the terms exactly.

An analyzer is typically used during indexing and searching. A full-text query will use mapping to search the analyzer and use it for each field. The analyzer can be used to look for a specific field, such as the following:

- An analyzer that is specified in the query
- The `search_analyzer` mapping parameters or analyzer
- An analyzer in the `default_search` or default index setting
- The `standard` analyzer

Anatomy of an analyzer

An analyzer is a package that contains three building blocks: **character filters, tokenizers,** and **token filters**. A user can create a custom analyzer by using these or other building blocks to create the functionality needed. Allow me to elaborate more on what these building blocks are:

- **Character filters** convert text into a stream of characters. They can transform the stream by adding, removing, or changing the format of the characters. For example, a character filer can change the & character to the word `and`. An analyzer may have no character filters, or many, but they are always applied in order.
- **Tokenizers** receive the stream of characters and break it down into tokens. The output will then be a stream of tokens. For example, a `whitespace` tokenizer breaks the text using whitespaces: `Hello World!` into `[hello, world]`. It also records the order of the terms, as well as the start and end character offsets of the original word that it represents. An analyzer must always contain only one tokenizer.
- **Token filters** are converters of token streams. They can add, remove, or even change the tokens. In the preceding example, notice how `Hello` became a lowercase word: `hello`. This change was performed by the token filter. Token filters cannot change the position or character offset of the tokens, and an analyzer can contain anywhere from zero to many token filters—and they are applied in order.

The following diagram shows how text is processed by an analyzer:

```
┌─────────────────────────────────────────────────────┐
│  ┌───────────────────────────────────────────────┐  │
│  │ <h2>Kibana</h2> is an Awesome Visualization Tool │  │
│  └───────────────────────────────────────────────┘  │
│                        │      ┌──────────────────┐   │
│                        ▼      │   html_strip     │   │
│                               │ character filter │   │
│  ┌───────────────────────────────────────────────┐  │
│  │    Kibana is an Awesome Visualization Tool      │  │
│  └───────────────────────────────────────────────┘  │
│                        │      ┌──────────────────┐   │
│                        ▼      │    Standard      │   │
│                               │    tokenizer     │   │
│  ┌───────────────────────────────────────────────┐  │
│  │ |Kibana| |is| |an| |Awesome| |Visualization| |Tool| │
│  └───────────────────────────────────────────────┘  │
│                        │      ┌──────────────────┐   │
│                        ▼      │    lowercase     │   │
│                               │   token filter   │   │
│  ┌───────────────────────────────────────────────┐  │
│  │ |kibana| |is| |an| |awesome| |visualization| |tool| │
│  └───────────────────────────────────────────────┘  │
└─────────────────────────────────────────────────────┘
```

In the preceding screenshot, we can see how the text **Kibana is an Awesome Visualization Tool** is processed by an Elasticsearch analyzer. As you can see, there are three steps involved:

1. The **html_strip character filter** strips the HTML tags.
2. The **Standard tokenizer** converts each word into tokens.
3. The **lowercase token filter** converts all uppercase tokens into lowercase.

This is the way the Elasticsearch analyzer works and indexes the data.

How to use an analyzer

In Elasticsearch, we have different options for character filters, tokenizers, and token filters and we can pick them as per the requirements. After applying the analyzer, we can find out how the analyzer is working by hitting the analyze API. The analyze API is important as it allows users to understand the terms that are produced by the analyzer.

The following example shows the analyze API for the `whitespace` analyzer:

```
POST _analyze
{
    "analyzer": "whitespace",
    "text": "It's not rocket science."
}
```

In the following expression, we are setting `tokenizer` and `filter` on the text:

```
POST _analyze
{
    "tokenizer": "standard",
    "filter": ["lowercase", "asciifolding"],
    "text": "Is this déja vu?"
}
```

Now, let's see about different types of analyzers available in Elasticsearch.

The custom analyzer

By using a `custom` analyzer, we can tweak the tokenizer and filter and more as per our requirement. This tweaking depends on the type of data we are playing with. A `custom` analyzer can be built to search on a specific index. Please refer to the following example, in which we are creating a custom analyzer:

```
PUT my_index_name
{
    "settings": {
        "analysis": {
            "analyzer": {
                "custom_analyzer": {
                    --define your custom analyzer
                    "type": "custom",
                    "tokenizer": "standard",
                    "filter": [
                        "lowercase",
                        "asciifolding"
                    ]
                }
            }
        }
    },
    "mappings": {
        "_doc": {
            "properties": {
```

```
                    "my_sentence": {
                        "type": "text",
                        "analyzer": "custom_analyzer"--the field my_sentence
     uses the custom analyzer
                    }
                }
            }
        }
    }
```

After applying the analyzer, we can search the data using the following query:

```
GET my_index_name / _analyze--refer to the custom analyzer {
    "analyzer": "custom_analyzer",
    --refer to the analyzer name "text": "Is this déjà vu?"
}

GET my_index_name / _analyze--refer to the custom analyzer {
    "field": "my_sentence",
    --refer to the custom analyzer by using the field name "text": "Is this
déjà vu?"
}
```

Elasticsearch uses a wide range of analyzers. The built-in analyzers are helpful as they do not require any further configuration, but sometimes the custom analyzers may be needed for complex or highly specific tasks.

The standard analyzer

If there is no analyzer specified, the standard analyzer will be chosen by default. It tokenizes the grammar based on the Unicode Text Segmentation; please refer to the following example:

```
POST _analyze
{
    "analyzer": "standard",
    "text": "This is my first program and these are my first 5 lines"
}
```

This will result in the following terms:

```
[first, program, these, 5, line]
```

The `standard` analyzer accepts the following parameters:

- The `max_token_length` parameter takes the token length and breaks it into intervals if it exceeds `255`.
- The `stopwords` parameter is a pre-defined stop list. By default, this is _none_. We can pass _english_ to handle English stop words; also, we can provide the array with a list of stop words.
- The `stopwords_path` parameter shows the path to the stop words file.

Let's look at the following example, in which we are setting `max_token_length` and `stopwords`:

```
PUT my_index
{
    "settings": {
        "analysis": {
            "analyzer": {
                "my_personalized_analyzer": {
                    "type": "standard",
                    "max_token_length": 5,
                    "stopwords": "_english_"
                }
            }
        }
    }
}
```

Now, let's check how this analyzer works by executing the analyze API:

```
POST my_index/_analyze
{
    "analyzer": "my_personalized_analyzer",
    "text": "This is my first program and these are my first 5 lines"
}
```

The `standard` analyzer consists of the `standard` tokenizer and two filters—a lowercase token filter and a stop token filter (which is disabled by default). To customize the `standard` analyzer, we must recreate it as a `custom` analyzer:

```
PUT standard_example
{
    "settings": {
        "analysis": {
            "analyzer": {
                "rebuilt_standard": {
                    "tokenizer": "standard",
```

```
                    "filter": [
                        "remove_duplicates"--add here any token filters
                    ]
                }
            }
        }
    }
}
```

The simple analyzer

A `simple` analyzer breaks the text into intervals whenever it encounters a non-letter term. It cannot be configured and only contains a `lowercase` tokenizer.

As you can see in the following simple analyzer example, we can add the filters that we want to use:

```
PUT simple_example
{
    "settings": {
        "analysis": {
            "analyzer": {
                "rebuilt_simple": {
                    "tokenizer": "lowercase",
                    "filter": [--add filter here]
                }
            }
        }
    }
}
```

The whitespace analyzer

A `whitespace` analyzer breaks the text into terms when it encounters whitespace characters:

```
POST _analyze
{
    "analyzer": "whitespace",
    "text": "This is my first program and these are my first 5 lines."
}
```

This will result in the following terms:

```
[this, is, my, first, program, and, these, are, my, first, 5, lines]
```

This analyzer cannot be configured. To alter it, users must create a `custom` analyzer that mimics the `whitespace` analyzer, and then add filters to it. As you can see in the following expression, we can add filters to the analyzer:

```
PUT whitespace_example
{
    "settings": {
        "analysis": {
            "analyzer": {
                "rebuilt_simple": {
                    "tokenizer": "whitespace",
                    "filter": [--add filter tokens here]
                }
            }
        }
    }
}
```

The stop analyzer

The `stop` analyzer is similar to the `simple` analyzer and adds support to remove stop words. By default, it will use _english_ stop words:

```
POST _analyze
{
    "analyzer": "stop",
    "text": "This is my first program and these are my first 5 lines."
}
```

This will result in the following terms:

```
[first, program, these, first, 5, lines]
```

Unlike the `whitespace` analyzer, the `stop` analyzer can be configured using the following:

- The `stopwords` parameter uses a pre-defined stop words list such as _english_ or an array of lists.
- The `stopwords_path` parameter points to the location of the file containing the stop words.

The `stop` analyzer can be configured to a `custom` analyzer as well:

```
PUT my_index_name
{
    "settings": {
        "analysis": {
            "analyzer": {
                "the_stop_analyzer": {
                    "type": "stop",
                    "stopwords": ["first", "and", "_english_"]
                }
            }
        }
    }
}
```

Now, let's check how this analyzer is working by hitting the `_analyze` endpoint:

```
POST my_index_name/_analyze
{
  "analyzer": "the_stop_analyzer",
  "text": "This is my first program and these are my first lines."
}
```

This will result in the following terms:

```
[my, program, my, lines]
```

The `stop` analyzer consists of a `lowercase` tokenizer as well as the stop token filter. To configure both parameters, simply create it as a `custom` analyzer:

```
PUT stop_example
{
    "settings": {
        "analysis": {
            "filter": {
                "english_stop": {
                    "type": "stop",
                    "stopwords": "_english_"--this can be overwritten with
stopwords or stopwords_path parameters
                }
            },
            "analyzer": {
                "rebuilt_stop": {
                    "tokenizer": "lowercase",
                    "filter": [
                        "english_stop"
                    ]
```

```
                }
              }
            }
          }
        }
```

The keyword analyzer

A `keyword` analyzer returns the entire string as a token:

```
POST _analyze
{
    "analyzer": "keyword",
    "text": "This is my first program and these are my first lines."
}
```

This will output the following result in a single term:

```
[This is my first program and these are my first lines.]
```

The `keyword` analyzer cannot be configured, and it consists of the `keyword` tokenizer. To customize the analyzer, it must be recreated and modified by adding token filters:

```
PUT keyword_example
{
    "settings": {
        "analysis": {
            "analyzer": {
                "rebuilt_keyword": {
                    "tokenizer": "keyword",
                    "filter": [--add filter here]
                }
            }
        }
    }
}
```

Using the preceding expression, we can modify the `keyword` analyzer by adding custom filters.

The pattern analyzer

A `pattern` analyzer splits the text into terms using a regular expression. The regular expression must match the token separators and not the tokens themselves. The regular expression defaults to non-word characters using `\W+`:

```
POST _analyze {
    "analyzer": "pattern",
    "text": "This is my first program and these are my first line."
}
```

This will output the following result, in a single term:

```
[this, is, my, first, program, and, these, are my first line.]
```

The `pattern` analyzer can be configured using the following:

- The `pattern` parameter defaults to `\W+`.
- The `flags` parameter represents Java flags.
- The `lowercase` parameter defaults all words to lowercase (the default is `true`).
- The `stopwords` parameter is a pre-defined stop words list such as `_english_` or an array of lists.
- The `stopwords_path` parameter points to the location of the file containing the stop words.

An example of configuration is setting the text to lowercase and removing all non-word characters:

```
PUT my_index_name
{
    "settings": {
        "analysis": {
            "analyzer": {
                "email_analyzer": {
                    "type": "pattern",
                    "pattern": "\\W|_",
                    "Lowercase": true
                }
            }
        }
    }
}
```

Now, let's check how this analyzer works by hitting the _analyze endpoint:

```
POST my_index_name/_analyze
{
  "analyzer": "email_analyzer",
  "text": "Jane_Smith@foo-bar.com"
}
```

This will output the following result:

```
[Jane, Smith, foo, bar, com]
```

The pattern analyzer consists of a pattern tokenizer, the lowercase token filter, and a stop token filter. A custom analyzer can be built by adding token filters:

```
PUT pattern_example
{
    "settings": {
        "analysis": {
            "tokenizer": {
                "split_on_non_word": {
                    "type": "pattern",
                    "pattern": "\\W+"
                }
            },
            "analyzer": {
                "rebuilt_pattern": {
                    "tokenizer": "split_on_non_word",
                    "filter": [
                        "lowercase"
                    ]
                }
            }
        }
    }
}
```

This way, we can create the analyzer by adding token filters.

The language analyzer

Language analyzers can be set to analyze the text of a specific language. They support custom stopwords, and the stem_exclusion parameter allows the user to specify a certain array of lowercase words that are not to be stemmed.

The fingerprint analyzer

The `fingerprint` analyzers implement a fingerprinting algorithm that allows clustering:

```
POST _analyze
{
 "analyzer": "fingerprint",
 "text": "Get busy living or get busy dying."
}
```

This will output the following result in a single term:

```
[busy dying get living or]
```

The `fingerprint` analyzer uses the following parameters:

- The `separator` parameter concatenates the terms using a character. By default, this is a space.
- The `max_output_size` parameter declares the maximum token size. By default, this is `255`.
- The `stopwords` parameter is a pre-defined stop words list such as `_english_` or an array of lists.
- The `stopwords_path` parameter points to the location of the file containing the stop words.

An example of configuration is shown as follows:

```
PUT my_index_name
{
    "settings": {
        "analysis": {
            "analyzer": {
                "fingerprint_analyzer": {
                    "type": "fingerprint",
                    "stopwords": "_english_"
                }
            }
        }
    }
}
```

Now, let's check how this analyzer is working by hitting the `_analyze` endpoint:

```
POST my_index_name/_analyze
{
    "analyzer": "fingerprint_analyzer",
```

```
            "text": "Get busy living or get busy dying."
    }
```

This will output the following result in a single term:

```
[ busy dying get living ]
```

To customize the `fingerprint` analyzer, the user needs to re-create it and add token filters to it.

Normalizers

Normalizers are a type of analyzer, but instead of producing multiple tokens, they only produce one. This is what distinguishes them from other types of analyzers. They do not contain tokenizers and accept only some character filters and token filters; the filters that can be used are `asciifolding`, `cjk_width`, `decimal_digit`, `elision`, `lowercase`, and `uppercase`, as well as some language filters. As with other analyzers, a custom normalization can be created:

```
PUT index
{
    "settings": {
        "analysis": {
            "char_filter": {
                "quote": {
                    "type": "mapping",
                    "mappings": [
                        "« => \"",
                        "» => \""
                    ]
                }
            },
            "normalizer": {
                "my_normalizer_name": {
                    "type": "custom",
                    "char_filter": ["quote"],
                    "filter": ["lowercase", "asciifolding"]
                }
            }
        }
    },
    "mappings": {
        "properties": {
            "foo": {
                "type": "keyword",
```

```
                            "normalizer": "my_normalizer_name"
                    }
                }
            }
        }
```

The preceding expression shows an example of creating a custom normalizer.

Tokenizers

A tokenizer receives a stream of characters from a string and, whenever it encounters whitespace, it outputs the characters as individual words known as tokens. A tokenizer is also in charge of keeping track of the order of each term and the start and end of character offsets. Various tokenizers can transform full text into individual words.

The standard tokenizer

The `standard` tokenizer uses Unicode Text Segmentation to divide the text. Consider the following example:

```
POST _analyze
{
    "tokenizer": "standard",
    "text": "Those who dare to fail miserably can achieve greatly."
}
```

This will output the following result:

```
[Those, who, dare, to, fail, miserably, can, achieve, greatly]
```

It accepts the `max_token_length` parameter, which will split the token if it exceeds the specified length. By default, this is set to `255`.

The letter tokenizer

The `letter` tokenizer breaks the text into individual words whenever it meets a character that is not a letter. This tokenizer is not configurable at all:

```
POST _analyze
{
    "tokenizer": "letter",
    "text": "You're a wizard, Harry."
}
```

This will output the following result:

```
[You, re, a, wizard, Harry]
```

The preceding tokens are generated through the letter tokenizer.

The lowercase tokenizer

The lowercase tokenizer, similar to the letter tokenizer, breaks the text into individual words whenever it finds a non-letter character, but it also turns all terms into lowercase:

```
POST _analyze
  {
    "tokenizer": "lowercase",
    "text": "You're a wizard, Harry."
  }
```

This will output the following result:

```
[you, re, a, wizard, harry]
```

Again, this tokenizer is not configurable.

The whitespace tokenizer

The whitespace tokenizer breaks the text into individual words whenever whitespace is encountered:

```
POST _analyze
  {
    "tokenizer": "lowercase",
    "text": "You're a wizard, Harry."
  }
```

This will output the following result:

```
[You're, a, wizard, Harry]
```

It accepts the max_token_length parameter, which will split the token if it exceeds the specified length, which again is set by default to 255.

The keyword tokenizer

The `keyword` tokenizer outputs the text as a single term:

```
POST _analyze
{
   "tokenizer": "keyword",
   "text": "Los Angeles"
}
```

This will output the following result:

```
[ Los Angeles ]
```

This tokenizer accepts the `buffer_size` parameter, which represents the number of characters read in a single pass. This is `256` by default.

The pattern tokenizer

The `pattern` tokenizer uses a regular expression to divide the text or capture the matching text as terms. The default pattern is `\W+`:

```
POST _analyze
{
   "tokenizer": "pattern",
   "text": "The foo_bar_size's default is 5."
}
```

This will output the following result:

```
[The, foo_bar_size, s, default, is, 5]
```

The `pattern` tokenizer can be configured using the following parameters:

- The `pattern` parameter defaults to `\W+`.
- The `flags` parameter represents Java flags.
- The `group` parameter captures the group as a token. By default, it splits at `-1`.

In the following example, the `pattern` tokenizer will break the text whenever it encounters a comma:

```
PUT my_index_name
{
    "settings": {
        "analysis": {
```

```
        "analyzer": {
            "my_analyzer_name": {
                "tokenizer": "my_tokenizer_name"
            }
        },
        "tokenizer": {
            "my_tokenizer_name": {
                "type": "pattern",
                "pattern": ","
            }
        }
    }
}
```

Now, let's check how this analyzer works by hitting the _analyze endpoint:

```
POST my_index_name/_analyze
{
    "analyzer": "my_analyzer_name",
    "text": "comma, separated, values"
}
```

This will output the following result:

```
[ comma, separated, values ]
```

The preceding tokens are created using comma as the pattern tokenizer.

The simple pattern tokenizer

The simple_pattern tokenizer uses a regular expression to divide the text or capture the matching text as terms, similar to the pattern tokenizer, but here, it only uses a pattern. It does not accept split patterns and is therefore generally faster than the pattern tokenizer. It accepts the pattern parameter, which defaults the text to an empty string.

The following example prints only the numbers, as long as they are three digits:

```
PUT my_index_name
{
    "settings": {
        "analysis": {
            "analyzer": {
                "my_analyzer_name": {
                    "tokenizer": "my_tokenizer_name"
                }
```

```
        },
        "tokenizer": {
            "my_tokenizer_name": {
                "type": "simple_pattern",
                "pattern": "[0123456789]{3}"
            }
        }
    }
}
```

Now let's check how this analyzer works by hitting the _analyze endpoint:

```
POST my_index_name/_analyze
{
    "analyzer": "my_analyzer_name",
    "text": "asta-313-267-847-mm-309"
}
```

This will output the following result:

```
[ 313, 267, 847, 309 ]
```

The preceding result shows the simple_pattern tokenizer output when we are extracting the output with a combination of three numbers.

Token filters

Token filters receive a stream of tokens from a tokenizer and have the ability to add, modify, or delete tokens. Important token filters include the following:

- The lowercase token filter normalizes the received text into lowercase tokens.
- The uppercase token filter normalizes the received text into uppercase tokens.
- The stop token filter removes the stop words from token streams.
- The reverse token filter reverses each token.
- The elision token filter removes elisions. For example, l'avion will be tokenized as avion.
- The truncate token filter cuts the tokens into specific lengths. By default, it's set to 10.
- The unique token filter indexes the unique tokens during analysis.
- The remove_duplicates token filter removes the tokens that are identical in the same position.

These can be configured with the following parameters:

- The `stopwords` parameter is a pre-defined stop words list such as `_english_` or an array of lists.
- The `stopwords_path` parameter points to the location of the file containing the stop words.
- The `ignore_case` parameter, set to `true`, will change all words into lowercase. By default, this is set to `false`.
- The `remove_trailing` parameter, set to `false`, will ignore the last term of a search if it is a stop word.

Character filters

Character filters process the stream of characters by adding, modifying, or removing characters before they are passed to the tokenizer. As seen previously in the `pattern` tokenizer, they can replace a pattern.

The HTML strip character filter

The `html_strip` character filter removes the HTML elements and decodes the HTML entities:

```
PUT my_index_name
{
    "settings": {
        "analysis": {
            "analyzer": {
                "my_analyzer_name": {
                    "tokenizer": "keyword",
                    "char_filter": ["my_char_filter_name"]
                }
            },
            "char_filter": {
                "my_char_filter_name": {
                    "type": "html_strip",
                    "escaped_tags": ["b"]
                }
            }
        }
    }
}
```

Now, let's check how this analyzer works by hitting the `_analyze` endpoint:

```
POST _analyze
{
    "tokenizer": "keyword",
    "char_filter": ["html_strip"],
    "text": "<p>I'm so <b>happy</b>!</p>"
}
```

This will output the following result as a single term:

```
[ \n I'm so happy! \n ]
```

This way we can strip the HTML tags using the `html_strip` character filter.

The mapping character filter

The `mapping` character filter accepts a map of keys and values that are then used to replace certain characters in a string with their associated keys. In the following example, this is used to transform Hindu-Arabic numerals into Arabic-Latin numbers:

```
PUT my_index_name {
    "settings": {
        "analysis": {
            "analyzer": {
                "my_analyzer_name": {
                    "tokenizer": "keyword",
                    "char_filter": [
                        "my_char_filter_name"
                    ]
                }
            },
            "char_filter": {
                "my_char_filter_name": {
                    "type": "mapping",
                    "mappings": [
                        "٠ => 0",
                        "١ => 1",
                        "٢ => 2",
                        "٣ => 3",
                        "٤ => 4",
                        "٥ => 5",
                        "٦ => 6",
                        "٧ => 7",
                        "٨ => 8",
                        "٩ => 9"
                    ]
```

```
            }
        }
    }
}
}
```

Now, let's check how this analyzer works by hitting the _analyze endpoint:

```
POST my_index_name/_analyze {
    "analyzer": "my_analyzer_name",
    "text": "My license plate is ٢٥٠١٥"
}
```

This will output the following result as a single term:

```
[ My license plate is 25015 ]
```

So, in this way, we can replace certain characters in a string with their associated keys.

The pattern replace character filter

The pattern_replace character filter searches with a regular expression and replaces the matched characters with the specified replacement string. An example of this was shown previously in the discussion of the custom analyzers.

Let's look at an example of configuring a custom analyzer build with the pattern_replace character filter:

```
PUT my_index_name
{
    "settings": {
        "analysis": {
            "analyzer": {
                "my_custom_analyzer_name": {
                    "type": "custom",
                    "tokenizer": "standard",
                    "char_filter": {
                        "my_char_filter": {
                            "type": "pattern_replace",
                            "pattern": """(\d+)-(?=\d)""",
                            "replacement": "$1_"
                        },
                        "filter": [
                            "lowercase",
                            "asciifolding"
                        ]
```

```
                                    }
                                }
                            }
                        }
                    }
                }
```

Now, let's check how this analyzer works by hitting the `_analyze` endpoint:

```
POST my_index_name/_analyze
{
  "analyzer": "my_custom_analyzer_name",
  "text": "My phone number is 102-456-789"
}
```

This will output the following result:

```
[ my, phone, number, is, 102_456_789 ]
```

This way we can use the `pattern_replace` character filter to modify the data as per the requirement. This was an example to understand the character filter. Now, we will move to the next section and will cover Elasticsearch mapping.

Mapping

Elasticsearch mapping is used to define the document structure with available fields and their datatypes. In Elasticsearch mapping, we have two types of fields, user-defined fields or properties and meta fields. User-defined fields can be any field that we use to provide for mapping or indexing while meta fields are those fields that help us to identify associated document metadata, for example, `_index`, `_id`, and `_source`.

Datatypes

Each field in an Elasticsearch document can have a datatype, and the datatype can be categorized into three categories, which are as follows.

The simple datatype

A simple datatype is used to represent text, numbers, Boolean values, or dates. We use `text`, `long`, `double`, `boolean`, `date`, and so on to represent these types.

The complex datatype

Complex datatypes are used to represent nested data, which is hierarchical. We use `object` or `nested` to represent these types of values.

The specialized datatype

With this type, we handle geo datatypes and such as `geo_shape` and `geo_point`.

Multi-field mapping

Multi-field mapping is a type of field mapping where we can map a field with different types. For example, we can index a string field with the text type, using which we can perform a full-text search. The same field can also be mapped as a keyword field, using which, we can easily perform sorting or data aggregation. In the same way, we can index a string field with different types of analyzers for different use cases. For example, in a text field, we can apply the `standard` analyzer and the `english` analyzer as well.

See the following example, where we are mapping the `ip_address` field with text as well as the keyword type:

```
{
    "index_name" : {
        "mappings" : {
            "_doc" : {
                "ip_address" : {
                    "full_name" : "ip_address",
                    "mapping" : {
                        "ip_address" : {
                            "type" : "text",
                            "fields" : {
                                "keyword" : {
                                    "type" : "keyword"
                                }
                            }
                        }
                    }
                }
            }
        }
    }
}
```

In the preceding example, using the `ip_address` field, we can perform a full-text search and we can easily perform sorting or data aggregation.

Elasticsearch mapping can be of two types, which are dynamic mapping and explicit mapping.

Dynamic mapping

In dynamic mapping, we need not define the datatypes before using it. As soon as we index the document, the mapping is created automatically. Elasticsearch does this dynamic mapping but sometimes the mapping goes wrong and in some cases, it assigns a string for a numeric value.

Explicit mapping

Although it is not required to create an explicit mapping because Elasticsearch does the dynamic mapping for us, sometimes, it is required to specify proper mapping before indexing and adding fields to the existing index. We can apply the explicit mapping using the create index API. See the following example, where we are using the create index API to create the explicit mapping:

```
PUT mappingtest
{
  "mappings": {
    "properties": {
      "name": {"type":"text"},
      "age": {"type": "integer"},
      "city":{"type":"text"}
    }
  }
}
```

In the preceding example, we are creating the `mappingtest` index and, in this index, we are creating the mapping for the `name`, `age`, and `city` fields. This way, we can create explicit mapping before indexing the actual document.

Summary

In this chapter, we covered text analysis and mapping, where we have gone through the anatomy of an analyzer in Elasticsearch. We introduced character filters, tokenizers, and token filters. We also covered how to use an analyzer and we have gone through different types of analyzers. After analyzers, we covered normalizers and tokenizers. Finally, we covered token filters and character filters.

In the next chapter, we will explore data searches in depth. We will cover URI search and body search.

5
Let's Do a Search!

Data searching is a very important aspect when we want to retrieve relevant information from a dataset. Sometimes, it is also important to understand the context before applying the actual search because if the context is incorrect, then we can return wrong and irrelevant data. Elasticsearch provides us with a variety of ways to tweak the search so that we can return the most relevant search results to the end users.

In this chapter, we will data search using Elasticsearch by delving into the following topics:

- Introduction to data search
- Search API

Introduction to data search

Elasticsearch provides a search option for queries, strings, and even bodies of text. Most search APIs are multi-index, meaning that they can be applied over multiple indices; the exception to multi-index will be explained in this chapter.

To illustrate searching properly, let's look at a specific example throughout this chapter—searching for a Facebook user. When performing a search, the `routing` parameter is used to point to the location of the shards in the indices that are to be searched. The following example will route to the user called `cactus_flower`:

```
POST facebook/_doc?routing=cactus_flower
{
  "user": "cactus_flower",
  "postDate": "2017-05-19T13:10:02",
  "message": "Just looking for the user Cactus Flower"
}
```

This search is known as a round-robin between replicas, where each replica is picked in the same rational order. To search for a more specific detail, such as the posts that are made by `cactus_flower`, we can write the following query:

```
POST /facebook/_doc?routing=cactus_flower
{
  "query": {
    "bool": {
      "must": {
        "query_string": {
          "query": "Posts created by cactus_flower"
        }
      },
      "filter": {
        "term": {
          "user": "cactus_flower"
        }
      }
    }
  }
}
```

As an alternative to the round-robin search replicas, an adaptive replica selection can be made. This will look for the **best** copy that the node can send the request to. There are a few criteria based on this method:

- The response time of the previous interactions between the coordinating node and the node that contains the copy of the data
- The extra time that the previous requests took to execute on the node containing the data
- The queue size of the requested data on the coordinating node

To activate this adaptive replica selection, the following setting needs to be changed to `true`:

```
cluster.routing.use_adaptive_replica_selection
```

We can change the preceding setting through a query as well. The following code shows how to implement this setting using the query:

```
PUT /_cluster/settings
{
  "transient": {
    "cluster.routing.use_adaptive_replica_selection": true
  }
}
```

Using the preceding query, we can set `cluster.routing.use_adaptive_replica_selection` to `true`.

In Elasticsearch, individual searches have timeout criteria. Elasticsearch will apply a global timeout to all the clusters that do not mention a timeout in their settings. To change these timeout settings, simply modify the `search.default_search_timeout` parameter and set a specific value. A value of `-1` will set the global search timeout to no timeout at all.

To cancel a search, the `_cancel` parameter is needed, along with the ID of the search task. Since searches on shards can be canceled, a large segment may lead to a delay in the cancellation. To minimize the cancel responsiveness, set `search.low_level_cancellation` to `true`. Please refer to the following example:

```
search.low_level_cancellation = true
```

By applying the preceding setting, we can enable `search.low_level_cancellation`.

The searches that are performed on Elasticsearch may need access to various shards simultaneously, and this will affect the CPU and memory. Users can limit the number of shards that can be accessed at once through the `max_concurrent_shard_requests` setting. This is a hard limit that can be set to any value. A soft limit can also be created using `action.search.shard_count.limit`.

Search API

The search API performs a search using a query string, a parameter, or a request body as the search criteria, and then it returns exact matches. The multi-index syntax is used by most search APIs to search over multiple indices, as follows:

- Users can search all of the documents in a specific index using the `cactus_flower` user:

  ```
  GET facebook/_search?q=user:cactus_flower
  ```

- This can also be applied using a tag:

  ```
  GET facebook/_search?q=tag:wow
  ```

- To search all the indices, use the `_all` tag instead of the index name:

  ```
  GET _all/_search?q=tag:wow
  ```

In the preceding query, we can query through all the available Elasticsearch indices for the tag using `wow`. Now, let's see how we can perform a URI-based search in Elasticsearch.

URI search

A URI search can be executed using a URI in the request parameters. This is used for a quick **curl test** using a simple search, but not all the search options are exposed:

```
GET facebook/_search?q=user:cactus_flower
```

The preceding URI query will output the following response:

```
{
  "took" : 25,
  "timed_out" : false,
  "_shards" : {
    "total" : 1,
    "successful" : 1,
    "skipped" : 0,
    "failed" : 0
  },
  "hits" : {
    "total" : {
      "value" : 1,
      "relation" : "eq"
    },
```

```
    "max_score" : 0.2876821,
    "hits" : [
      {
        "_index" : "facebook",
        "_type" : "_doc",
        "_id" : "mgHGpGsBtpBTvATzpKN4",
        "_score" : 0.2876821,
        "_routing" : "cactus_flower",
        "_source" : {
          "user" : "cactus_flower",
          "postDate" : "2017-05-19T13:10:02",
          "message" : "Just looking for the user Cactus Flower"
        }
      }
    ]
  }
}
```

The parameters that were used in the URI search are as follows:

- q: The query string.
- df: The default field to be used when nothing is defined.
- analyzer: The analyzer name that was used to execute the search.
- analyze_wildcard: Checks whether a wildcard and prefix queries are to be analyzed. The default is set to false.
- batched_reduced_size: The number of shards that will be reduced on the coordinating node. This is used to void memory overhead per search request.
- default_operator: The default operator that is to be used. The default is OR and it can be set to AND.
- lenient: Ignores format-based failures. It defaults to false.
- explain: Contains information on how the scoring of the hit was computed. It does this for every hit.

- stored_fields: Retrieves the selective store fields of the documents that were retrieved with each hit. When no value is indicated, it will show no fields in the returned hits.
- sort: Performs sorting and is written as fieldName or fieldName:asc/ fieldName:dec. It can be an actual field name or a special _score name.
- track_scores: Defaults to true and tracks the scores when sorting. It will return this with the hits.
- track_total_hits: Defaults to false and tracks the total number of hits that match the query.

- `timeout`: A search timeout that's used to execute the search within a specified time. It defaults to no timeout.
- `terminate_after`: Will retrieve whether the query execution was terminated early. It defaults to no terminate_after.
- `from`: The number of the index that will start the return values. It defaults to 0.
- `size`: The number of hits to be returned. It defaults to 10.
- `search_type`: Determines which type of search operation is to be executed. It can be `dfs_query_then_fetch` or `query_then_fetch`.
- `allow_partial_search_results`: If this is set to `false`, any partial results will mean an overall failure. This is controlled with `search.default_allow_partial_results`.

Request body search

Search requests are executed with a search DSL. The following example shows the Query DSL within the request body:

```
GET /facebook/_search
{
  "query": {
    "term": {
      "user": "cactus_flower"
    }
  }
}
```

The preceding query will return the following response:

```
{
  "took" : 2,
  "timed_out" : false,
  "_shards" : {
    "total" : 1,
    "successful" : 1,
    "skipped" : 0,
    "failed" : 0
  },
  "hits" : {
    "total" : {
      "value" : 1,
      "relation" : "eq"
    },
    "max_score" : 0.2876821,
```

```
    "hits" : [
       {
         "_index" : "facebook",
         "_type" : "_doc",
         "_id" : "mgHGpGsBtpBTvATzpKN4",
         "_score" : 0.2876821,
         "_routing" : "cactus_flower",
         "_source" : {
           "user" : "cactus_flower",
           "postDate" : "2017-05-19T13:10:02",
           "message" : "Just looking for the user Cactus Flower"
         }
       }
    ]
  }
}
```

The parameters for the body search are as follows:

- timeout: If set, this means that searches must be executed within a specified time. It defaults to no timeout.
- from: The number of the index from which to start the return values. It defaults to 0.
- size: The number of hits to be returned. It defaults to 10.
- search_type: Determines which type of search operation is to be executed. It can be dfs_query_then_fetch or query_then_fetch.
- request_cache: If set to true, it enables the caching of search requests with aggregations and suggestions (known as size = 0).
- allow_partial_search_results: If the request returns partial results, this will result in an overall failure if this parameter is set to false. This can be controlled with the search.default_allow_partial_results setting.
- terminate_after: This will specify whether the query execution was terminated early. It defaults to no terminate_after.
- batched_reduced_size: The number of shards that will be reduced on the coordinating node. This is used to void memory overhead per search request.

The search_type, allow_partial_search_results, and request_cache parameters are set as query string parameters. The others are passed within the body. Searches within the body are allowed with HTTP, GET, and POST.

Query

Now, let's discuss the body search in more detail. This is where we pass the query using the `query` keyword. The query element defines a query in the request body using Query DSL:

```
GET /_search
{
  "query": {
    "term": {
      "user": "cactus_flower"
    }
  }
}
```

In the preceding query, we are executing the `term` query, which we are using to match the user field against `cactus_flower`.

From/size

The search query can be modified to return only a specific set of indices or a number of hits using the `from` and `size` parameters in the expression, as shown in the following code:

```
GET /_search
{
  "from" : 0, "size" : 10,
  "query": {
    "term": {
      "user": "cactus_flower"
    }
  }
}
```

The from size and the overall size cannot be greater than the `index.max_result_window` index setting (which defaults to 10,000).

Sort

The sort element allows us to sort the results on specific fields. Each sort is reversible. To sort by score, the _score field name is used, whereas to sort by an index, the _doc field name is used. The following is an example of index mapping:

```
PUT /my_index
{
  "mappings": {
```

```
    "_doc": {
      "properties": {
        "post_date": {
          "type": "date"
        },
        "user": {
          "type": "keyword"
        },
        "name": {
          "type": "keyword"
        },
        "age": {
          "type": "integer"
        }
      }
    }
  }
}
```

Using the following query, we can retrieve all the posts that were created by
cactus_flower. Here, we are sorting the result using the post_date field and setting the
sort order to ascending:

```
GET /my_index/_search
{
  "sort": [
    {
      "post_date": {
        "order": "asc"
      }
    },
    "user",
    {
      "name": "desc"
    },
    {
      "age": "desc"
    },
    "_score"
  ],
  "query": {
    "term": {
      "user": "cactus_flower"
    }
  }
}
```

The `order` option can be one of the following:

- `asc`: Sorts in ascending order
- `desc`: Sorts in descending order

`_score` defaults to `desc`, whereas everything else defaults to `asc`. The `mode` option controls the array value to be chosen for the sorting document:

- `min`: Chooses the lowest value.
- `max`: Chooses the highest value.
- `sum`: Chooses the sum of all the values as a sort value. This is only for number-based array fields.
- `avg`: Chooses the average of all the values as a sort value. This is only for number-based array fields.
- `median`: Chooses the median of all the values as a sort value. This is only for number-based array fields.

Let's look at an example of sorting. Let's add a document with a `price` field so that we can sort on that:

```
PUT /my_index/_doc/1?refresh
{
  "product": "candy",
  "price": [
    15,
    3
  ]
}
```

The preceding query will add the document. Now, we will sort the results with `price` using the following query:

```
POST /my_index/_search
{
  "query": {
    "term": {
      "product": "candy"
    }
  },
  "sort": [
    {
      "price": {
        "order": "asc",
        "mode": "avg"
      }
```

```
      }
    ]
  }
```

Elasticsearch supports sorting in nested objects as well. The nested option has the following properties:

- path: Defines the path to the nested object.
- filter: A filter that the inner objects need to pass through before being considered.
- max_children: The maximum number of children per root document. It defaults to unlimited.
- nested: Applies to another nested path within the nested object.

Source filtering

This controls how the _source field is returned with each hit, and it defaults to true:

```
GET /_search
{
  "_source": false,
  "query": {
    "term": {
      "user": "cactus_flower"
    }
  }
}
```

It also accepts wildcards:

```
GET /_search
{
  "_source": "obj.*",
  "query": {
    "term": {
      "user": "cactus_flower"
    }
  }
}
```

To have more specific search control, the pattern's includes and excludes can be used:

```
GET /_search
{
  "_source": {
    "includes": [
      "obj1.*",
      "obj2.*"
    ],
    "excludes": [
      "*.description"
    ]
  },
  "query": {
    "term": {
      "user": "cactus_flower"
    }
  }
}
```

In the preceding query, we can include or exclude the fields from the result.

Fields

The `stored_fields` parameter is off by default and is not recommended. Source filtering is recommended instead.

Script fields

Script fields return a script evaluation for each hit. They are applied to fields that are not stored and allow the evaluated value of the script to be returned. They can also access the document's source and extract specific elements with `params['_source']`. The following example shows _source pointing to the JSON-like model:

```
GET /_search
{
  "query": {
    "match_all": {}
  },
  "script_fields": {
    "test1": {
      "script": "params['_source']['message']"
    }
  }
}
```

Doc value fields

This field returns the doc value representation of a field for each hit. They are applied to fields that have doc values, regardless of whether they are stored:

```
GET /_search
{
  "query": {
    "match_all": {}
  },
  "docvalue_fields": [
    {
      "field": "*_date_field", -- matched all fields that end with field
      "format": "epoch_millis" -- the format to be applied to the fields
    }
  ]
}
```

Date fields and numeric fields are some of the only fields that accept custom formats.

Post filter

The post filter is applied to the hits that are returned after a search request. Let's create the chocolates index, which will include the brand, flavours, and taste fields. We will use this index to explain the post filter:

```
PUT /chocolates
{
  "mappings": {
    "properties": {
      "brand": {
        "type": "keyword"
      },
      "flavours": {
        "type": "keyword"
      },
      "taste": {
        "type": "keyword"
      }
    }
  }
}
```

The preceding expression creates the chocolates index. Now, let's add a certain type of chocolate with the company's information. To do that, we need to execute the following query:

```
PUT /chocolates/_doc/1?refresh
{
  "brand": "milka",
  "flavours": "dark chocolate",
  "taste": "salty"
}
```

The preceding expression adds a document to the chocolates index. In the same way, we can add documents with different brands, flavors, and tastes. Now, we can retrieve all of the chocolates from milka that are marked as salty. It uses term aggregation to do this:

```
GET /chocolates/_search
{
  "query": {
    "bool": {
      "filter": [
        {
          "term": {
            " flavours ": "red"
          }
        },
        {
          "term": {
            "brand": "milka"
          }
        }
      ]
    }
  },
  "aggs": {
    "tastes": {
      "terms": {
        "field": "salty"
      }
    }
  }
}
```

In the preceding query, we fetched the results and aggregated it with tastes as salty.

Highlighting

Highlighters permit the highlighting of snippets from one or more fields:

```
GET /_search
{
  "query": {
    "match": {
      "content": "cactus_flower"
    }
  },
  "highlight": {
    "fields": {
      "content": {}
    }
  }
}
```

The highlighters are specified in the highlighter type and they can be unified, plain, or a **fast vector highlighter** (**FVH**). Let's go over what they do:

- The unified highlighter uses the Lucene Unified highlighter and breaks the text into sentences by using the BM25 algorithm.
- The plain highlighter uses the standard Lucene highlighter. It returns the reflect query logic.
- The fvh highlighter uses the Lucene fvh. It can be customized using boundary_scanner and requires setting term_vector to with_position_offsets in order to increase the size of the index. It can also combine multiple fields and can be used to assign weights to different positions to modify the order of importance of a query.

The parameters that are used by highlight fields are as follows:

- boundary_chars: A string that contains the boundary characters. Defaults to .,!?\t\n.
- boundary_max_scan: The range of the boundary characters. Defaults to 20.
- boundary_scanner_locale: This controls which locale is used for searches.
- encoder: Specifies whether the snippet should be HTML encoded and is either default or html.
- fields: Specifies the fields that are to be retrieved for highlighting.
- force_source: Highlights the source of the field. Defaults to false.

- `fragmenter`: Indicates how the text is to be broken in snippets. It can be `simple` or `span`.
- `fragment_offset`: This controls which end of the range to start highlighting. Only available in the `fvh` highlighter.
- `fragment_size`: Specifies the size of the highlighted fragment in characters. Defaults to `100`.
- `highlight_query`: Highlights the matches for a different query.
- `matched_fields`: Combines multiple fields and highlights a single field.
- `no_match_size`: The amount of text to be returned from the beginning of the field in the case where there are no matching fragments. Defaults to `0`.
- `number_of_fragments`: Specifies the maximum number of fragments to be returned. Defaults to `5`.
- `order`: Sorts the highlighted hits. The score value will sort according to the score of the hit. Defaults to `5`.
- `phrase_limit`: Indicates the number of matching phrases within a document to be considered. It helps prevent `fvh` from analyzing too many phrases and affecting memory.
- `pre_tags`: Defines the HTML tags. Used in conjunction with `post_tags`. By default, the text is wrapped with `<em>` and `</em>` tags.
- `post_tags`: Defines the HTML tags. Used in conjunction with `pre_tags`. By default, the text is wrapped with `<em>` and `</em>` tags.
- `require_field_match`: Highlights only the fields that match the query. If set to `false`, it will highlight all fields. It defaults to `true`.
- `tags_schema`: Sets to the styled schema to define `pre_tags` and `post_tags`.
- `type`: Indicates the type of highlighter to be used, that is, `unified`, `plain`, or `fvh`.

Rescoring

Rescoring helps with the precision of requests by reordering the search hits. It is used in the `query` and `post_filter` phases:

```
POST /_search
{
  "query": {
    "match": {
      "message": {
        "operator": "or",
```

```
          "query": "the quick brown"
        }
      }
    },
    "rescore": {
      "window_size": 50,
      "query": {
        "rescore_query": {
          "match_phrase": {
            "message": {
              "query": "the quick brown",
              "slop": 2
            }
          }
        },
        "query_weight": 0.7,
        "rescore_query_weight": 1.2
      }
    }
  }
}
```

The parameters are as follows:

- `total`: Sum the original score and the rescore query score
- `multiply`: Multiply the original score and the rescore query score
- `avg`: The average of the original score and the rescore query score
- `max`: The maximum of the original score and the rescore query score
- `min`: The minimum of the original score and the rescore query score

Search type

Searches can be executed using different paths. The distribution search operation is scattered to all the relevant shards, and then the results are retrieved. It will sort through the results and check for correctability. Since each shard is independent, the searches of term frequencies happen over all the shards. To provide an accurate ranking, the term frequencies of the shards need to be used to calculate a global term frequency, which will then be applied to the query in each shard search.

Elasticsearch allows control over the type of search to be performed on a per search request basis. The settings are configured in the `search_type` parameter in the query string. The first setting that can be used is the `query_then_fetch` value. This will send the query to all the shards that are relevant. Each shard performs the search and returns the necessary information to the coordinating node, which will merge and resort the results from all the shards it contains. The second value that can be used is `dfs_query_then_fetch`. This is very similar to `query_then_fetch`, except that it provides more accurate scoring.

Scroll

The scroll API retrieves a large number of results. The `scroll` field is used to scroll through large amounts of data, that is, more than 10,000 search results, and is not intended to be used for real-time user requests.

Preference

This controls the preference of the shard copies that are used to execute the search. It can be set to any of the following:

- `_only_local`: Only local shards that have been allocated to the local node are used to execute the operation.
- `_local`: Only shards that are from the local node are used to execute the operation, and the process falls back to other shards when this is not possible.
- `_prefer_nodes: abc, xyz`: Executes the operation on those nodes if possible.
- `_shards: 2, 3`: Restricts operation to the specified shards.
- `_only_nodes: abc*, x*yz, …`: Restricts operation to the specified nodes.

Explanation

This will print an explanation of the query regarding how each hit was computed:

```
GET /_search
{
  "explain": true,
  "query": {
    "term": {
      "user": "cactus_flower"
    }
  }
}
```

Version

This returns a version for each result hit:

```
GET /_search
{
  "version": true,
  "query": {
    "term": {
      "user": "cactus_flower"
    }
  }
}
```

The preceding query will return the version number, along with the results.

min_score

`min_score` excludes documents that do not meet the minimum score specified:

```
GET /_search
{
  "min_score": 0.5,
  "query": {
    "term": {
      "user": "cactus_flower"
    }
  }
}
```

The preceding query will return only those records where the score is more than `0.5`, as specified for `min_score`.

Named queries

Using _name, we can define a name for each filter and query:

```
GET /_search
{
  "query": {
    "bool": {
      "should": [
        {
          "match": {
            "name.first": {
              "query": "John",
```

```
            "_name": "first"
          }
        }
      },
      {
        "match": {
          "name.last": {
            "query": "Smith",
            "_name": "last"
          }
        }
      }
    ],
    "filter": {
      "terms": {
        "name.last": [
          "Smith",
          "cactus_flower"
        ],
        "_name": "test"
      }
    }
  }
}
```

In the preceding expression, we are giving a name to the filter by using _name.

Inner hits

These are used for nested and parent-join documents that match. In the case of parent/child, the parent documents are retrieved on matches in the child documents, while child documents are returned in the match of parent documents. The inner hits feature is used to determine exactly which inner nested object or parent/child document matches the search query. The query has the following format:

```
"<query>": {
  "inner_hits": {
    <inner_hits_options>
  }
}
```

Here, the options are as follows:

- from: The first hit to fetch inner_hits.
- size: The maximum number of hits per inner_hits.

- `sort`: What type of sorting should take place. Defaults to sorting by score.
- `name`: Defines the name for the inner hit definition.

Field collapsing

This allows the search to collapse according to the field values. Choosing the top sorted document per collapse key will result in a collapse. In the following example, the best tweets per user are being retrieved and sorted by the number of likes:

```
GET /twitter/_search
{
  "query": {
    "match": {
      "message": "elasticsearch"
    }
  },
  "collapse": {
    "field": "user"
  },
  "sort": [
    "likes"
  ],
  "from": 10
}
```

In the preceding example, we are collapsing the `user` field.

Search template

The search template API allows for the use of the mustache language to prerender search actions before they are executed:

```
GET _search/template
{
  "source": {
    "query": {
      "match": {
        "{{my_field}}": "{{my_value}}"
      }
    },
    "size": "{{my_size}}"
  },
  "params": {
    "my_field": "message",
```

```
        "my_value": "some message",
        "my_size": 5
    }
}
```

In the preceding example, we are filling the existing templates with template parameters.

Multi search template

The multi search template allows for the execution of the search over multiple template requests in the same API. It does this by using the _msearch/template endpoint. It is similar in format to the multi search API. The structure of the multi search template is as follows:

```
header\n
body\n
header\n
body\n
```

As seen in the preceding example, each newline character ends with \n. Each line may be preceded by \r. The header indicates which indices are to be searched, that is, search_type, preference, and routing:

```
$ cat requests
{"index": "test"}
{"source": {"query": {"match": {"user" : "{{username}}" }}}, "params":
{"username": "John"}}
{"source": {"query": {"{{query_type}}": {"name": "{{name}}" }}}, "params":
{"query_type": "match_phrase_prefix", "name": "Smith"}}
{"index": "_all"}
{"id": "template_1", "params": {"query_string": "search for these words" }}
```

Using the preceding expression, we can perform multiple searches at once.

Search shards API

The search shards API retrieves the indices and shards that the search request is executed on. This is used to get feedback and determine issues, plan optimizations, or determine shard preference. The following is an example of this:

```
GET /twitter/_search_shards
```

This will output information about all the nodes in the `twitter` index. To specify a route, add the `routing` parameter with the path to the search shard API:

```
GET /twitter/_search_shards?routing=foo,bar
```

The search shard API uses the following parameters:

- `routing`: A list of comma-separated values to determine the location of the shards to be searched during execution.
- `preference`: Gives preference to shard replicas. Defaults to random.
- `local`: A Boolean value that determines whether to read the cluster locally.

Suggesters

The suggest feature looks for similar terms based on the suggested text. `_suggesters` has been deprecated and `_search` is now used instead.

Multi search API

The multi search API allows for the execution of search requests within the same API:

```
$ cat requests
{"index":"test"}
{"query":{"match_all":{}},"from":0,"size":10}
{"index":"test","search_type":"dfs_query_then_fetch"}
{"query":{"match_all":{}}}
{}
{"query":{"match_all":{}}}
{"query"  :  {"match_all":{}}}
{"search_type":"dfs_query_then_fetch"}
{"query":{"match_all":{}}}
```

The header indicates which indices are to be searched, that is, `search_type`, `preference`, and `routing`.

Count API

The count API executes a query and retrieves the number of matches within that query. The query can be defined using a query string as a parameter or using Query DSL:

```
GET /facebook/_count
{
  "query": {
    "term": {
      "user": "cactus_flower"
    }
  }
}
```

It can be applied to multiple indices. The `request` parameters can be any of the following:

- `df`: The default field to be used.
- `analyzer`: The name of the analyzer that's used to analyze the query string.
- `default_operator`: The default operator to be used. The default is `OR` and can be set to `AND`.
- `lenient`: Ignores format-based failures. It defaults to `false`.
- `analyze_wildcard`: Indicates whether a wildcard and prefix queries are to be analyzed. The default is `false`.
- `terminate_after`: Will retrieve whether the query's execution was terminated early. It defaults to no terminate_after.

The request body count can use Query DSL to express which query should be executed. The body content can be passed as a source through the `REST` parameter.

Note that the count operation is applied across all shards. It will select the replica for each shard ID group and perform a search against it. A routing value can be specified to identify which shards to execute the count request on.

Validate API

The validate API validates a potentially expensive query without executing it. It uses the following parameters:

- `df`: The default field to be used.
- `analyzer`: The name of the analyzer that's used to analyze the query string.

- default_operator: The default operator to be used. The default is OR and can be set to AND.
- lenient: Ignores format-based failures. It defaults to false.
- analyze_wildcard: Indicates whether a wildcard and prefix queries are to be analyzed. The default is set to false.

In the following example, the validation of the query will be tested:

```
PUT twitter/_bulk?refresh
{"index":{"_id":1}}
{"user" : "cactus_flower", "post_date" : "2009-11-15T14:12:12", "message" :
"trying out Elasticsearch"}
{"index":{"_id":2}}
{"user" : "cactus_pot", "post_date" : "2009-11-15T14:12:13", "message" :
"My username is similar to @cactus_flower!"}
```

To test the query, use the following query:

```
GET twitter/_validate/query?q=user:foo
```

The resulting output is as follows:

```
{"valid":true,"_shards":{"total":1,"successful":1,"failed":0}}
```

Explain API

The explain API explains the score computation of a query and a document:

```
GET /twitter/_explain/0
{
  "query": {
    "match": {
      "message": "elasticsearch"
    }
  }
}
```

Here, we have the following parameters

- _source: Retrieves the source if set to true.
- stored_fields: Controls which stored fields are returned as part of the document being explained.
- routing: When routing is used during indexing, this will control the routing.
- parent: This is the same as routing.

- `preference`: Controls which shard the explain is executed on.
- `source`: The data of the request will be put in the query string.
- `df`: The default field to be used.
- `q`: The query string.
- `analyzer`: The analyzer that's being used.
- `default_operator`: The default operator. The default is `OR` and can be set to `AND`.
- `lenient`: Ignores format-based failures. It defaults to `false`.
- `analyze_wildcard`: Indicates whether a wildcard and prefix queries are to be analyzed. The default is set to `false`.

Profile API

The Profile API is a debugging tool. It adds detailed information about the execution of each component in a search request. It gives the user insight about every step a search request performs and can assist in determining why certain requests are slow.

A `_search` request can be profiled by adding the top-level `profile` parameter:

```
GET /twitter/_search
{
  "profile": true,
  "query": {
    "match": {
      "message": "some number"
    }
  }
}
```

Profiling queries

The Profile API on queries exposes Lucene class names and concepts. This requires some knowledge of Lucene:

- The query section contains detailed timing that's executed by Lucene on a shard.
- The breakdown component lists the timing statistics about the low-level execution.
- The collectors section shows the high-level execution details.
- The rewrite section performs optimizations. This is a very complex process.

Profiling aggregations

The aggregations section contains detailed information about the timing of the aggregation tree that's executed by a shard.

Profiling considerations

When using the Profile API, a non-negligible overhead is added to the search execution, and this leads to a number of limitations.

Profiling does not measure the search fetch phase, nor the network overhead. It also doesn't account for the time spent in the queue, merging, or doing any additional work. The statistics are not available for suggestions, highlighting, or `dfs_query_then_fetch`. It is a highly experimental instrument and a part of Lucene that is used for diagnostics.

Field capabilities API

This retrieves the capabilities of fields among multiple indices.

To execute on all indices, use the following query:

```
GET _field_caps?fields=rating
```

To execute on a specific index, use the following query:

```
GET twitter/_field_caps?fields=rating
```

The parameters are as follows:

- `searchable`: Whether the field is indexed for search on all indices
- `aggregatable`: Whether the field can be aggregated on all indices
- `indices`: A list of indices where the field is of the same type
- `non_searchable_indices`: A list of indices where searches cannot be executed
- `non_aggregatable_indices`: A list of indices where the field is not aggregatable

The request for the response format is as follows:

```
GET _field_caps?fields=rating,title
{
  "fields": {
    "rating": {
```

```
      "long": { -- defined as long for index 1 and 2
        "searchable": true,
        "aggregatable": false,
        "indices": [
          "index1",
          "index2"
        ],
        "non_aggregatable_indices": [
          "index1"
        ]
      },
      "keyword": { -- defined as keyword for index 3 and 4
        "searchable": false,
        "aggregatable": true,
        "indices": [
          "index3",
          "index4"
        ],
        "non_searchable_indices": [
          "index4"
        ]
      }
    },
    "title": {
      "text": {
        "searchable": true,
        "aggregatable": false
      }
    }
  }
}
```

In the preceding query response, the field rating is defined as `long`.

Summary

In this chapter, we have learned about data search in Elasticsearch. We covered URI search and body search so that we could explain how we can perform these searches. Then we covered query examples using term, from/size, sort, and source filtering. We also covered highlighting, rescoring, search type, and named queries. After that, we covered the APIs for the search shard, multi search, count, validate, explain, Profile, and field capabilities.

In the next chapter, we will cover data sparsity and how to improve the performance of Elasticsearch.

6
Performance Tuning

In this chapter, we will look into Elasticsearch performance-related issues and how we can tweak Elasticsearch to get the maximum output. Elasticsearch is widely used to search through a database and return documents that match the query, but it can quickly become overwhelmed when it has to retrieve a large number of documents using a single query. The Scroll API is therefore recommended in these situations. Elasticsearch does not index documents larger than 100 MB, but this setting can be changed in `http.max_content_length` as long as it does not go over the Lucene limit of 2 GB. Generally, users are recommended to avoid using large documents in Elasticsearch, as they put stress on the network and overwhelm memory usage and disk space.

In this chapter, we are going to cover the following topics:

- Data sparsity
- Solutions to common problems
- How to tune for indexing speed
- How to tune for search speed
- How to tune search queries with the Profile API
- How to tune for disk usage

Data sparsity

In previous versions of Elasticsearch, the sparsity of documents was to be avoided because of Lucene's structure. This structure identifies documents internally with document IDs, which are then used for communication between the internal APIs of Lucene. Lucene retrieves values of the norm from the document ID, generated by a search query, by reading the byte at the index of the document ID.

 Lucene is a full-featured text search engine that is written in Java, and Elasticsearch is built on top of Lucene.

This is, at the same time, both very efficient and time-intensive, because Lucene can quickly access the norm values and the documents that have no value and use one byte of storage for each. This means, though, that if an index has **x** documents, the norms require **x** bytes of storage per field. This not only affects the sparsity requirements, but also the indexing speed and the search speed. The documents that have no field would still be written at an index time and then skipped over sparsity.

To avoid data sparsity, a range of changes can be performed. Some of these changes avoid allocating unrelated data to the same index. Others normalize the document structure and set the same field name for the same data. In sparse fields, it's best to avoid using the norm and `doc_values`. Another point to note about indexing and documents is the importance of deciding what the unit of information should be. To be able to search within books, it might be better to use each chapter as a document, and not the entire books themselves as documents. So, here we can group similar content in different chapters, which makes searching for any topic within a chapter easy, instead of looking in the entire book. The same logic applies to the documents as well. The documents (the chapters they contain) can then contain a property that attributes them to a specific book. Data sparsity had been taken out of Elasticsearch version 7, minimizing the possibility of this issue.

Solutions to common problems

We have discussed the common issues that we face with Elasticsearch, but there are ways in which we can avoid these issues. So, let's take a look at how to fix some common problems.

Mixing exact search with stemming

When building a search query, stemming is a necessary component. Stemming is the process of reducing words to their root form—as shown throughout the examples in Chapter 3, *Many as One – the Distributed Model*. For example, when looking for **paid**, your search may return **pay**, **paid**, and **paying**. To be able to return the word **paid** specifically, we can use a multi-field. I have explained multi-fields in Chapter 4, *Prepping Your Data – Text Analysis and Mapping*. In the following example, we are creating the index with the english analyzer:

```
PUT index
{
  "settings": {
    "analysis": {
      "analyzer": {
        "english_exact": {
          "tokenizer": "standard",
          "filter": [
            "lowercase"
          ]
        }
      }
    }
  },
  "mappings": {
    "properties": {
      "body": {
        "type": "text",
        "analyzer": "english",
        "fields": {
          "exact": {
            "type": "text",
            "analyzer": "english_exact"
          }
        }
      }
    }
  }
}
```

By using the preceding expression, we can create an index. After creating the index, let's add some documents so that we can perform the search on the index:

```
PUT index/_doc/1
{
"body": "The pay should be done through a local bank deposit."
}
```

```
PUT index/_doc/2
{
"body": "The payment has been received."
}
```

After adding the document, let's refresh the index using the following expression:

```
POST index/_refresh
```

These two documents are set up with different bodies. To search for `pay` in the documents, we can use the following query:

```
GET index/_search
{
   "query": {
     "simple_query_string": {
        "fields": [
          "body"
        ],
        "query": "pay"
     }
   }
}
```

The preceding query will return the following response:

```
{
   "took" : 0,
   "timed_out" : false,
   "_shards" : {
     "total" : 1,
     "successful" : 1,
     "skipped" : 0,
     "failed" : 0
   },
   "hits" : {
     "total" : {
        "value" : 2,
        "relation" : "eq"
     },
     "max_score" : 0.18232156,
     "hits" : [
        {
          "_index" : "index",
          "_type" : "_doc",
          "_id" : "1",
          "_score" : 0.18232156,
          "_source" : {
```

```
        "body" : "The pay should be done through a local bank deposit."
      }
    },
    {
      "_index" : "index",
      "_type" : "_doc",
      "_id" : "2",
      "_score" : 0.18232156,
      "_source" : {
        "body" : "The payment has been received."
      }
    }
  ]
}
}
```

A search for pay on body.exact will return only one document, as shown in the following
expression:

```
GET index/_search
{
  "query": {
    "simple_query_string": {
      "fields": [
        "body.exact"
      ],
      "query": "pay"
    }
  }
}
```

The preceding query will return the following response:

```
{
    "took": 1,
    "timed_out": false,
    "_shards": {
        "total": 1,
        "successful": 1,
        "skipped": 0,
        "failed": 0
    },
    "hits": {
        "total": {
            "value": 1,
            "relation": "eq"
        },
        "max_score": 0.8025915,
```

```
        "hits": [
            {
                "_index": "index",
                "_type": "_doc",
                "_id": "1",
                "_score": 0.8025915,
                "_source": {
                    "body": "The pay should be done through a local bank
deposit."
                }
            }
        ]
    }
]
}
```

In the preceding result, we are getting a single result as we are matching the exact word pay in the query.

Inconsistent scoring

The scoring in Elasticsearch varies, and shards and replicas make it even more complex. When a user runs the same request twice in a row, the scoring of the documents may come back different. This is because of replicas. Elasticsearch selects the shards that are to be used for the query, and it is very possible that it will not choose the same shards for the same task each time.

Scoring is related to index statistics, and index statistics depends on shards, how the documents are updated or deleted, and whether there is a delay in deleting a document (for example, when setting delete to occur the next time the shard is used for merging). The deleted documents are taken into account when looking at the index statistics. The recommended workaround is to use a string that sets the user as a preference and ensures that the queries of this user will always use the same shards—leading to consistent scoring. Another advantage of this is that when two documents return the same score, they will be sorted by the internal Lucene document ID.

A problem might arise when two documents with the same content have different scores. This also happens because of sharding, as Elasticsearch makes each shard responsible for its own score. It is assumed that event-routed shards lead to similar index statistics. Fixing this on a small dataset requires indexing everything into a single shard. On large datasets, this is unfeasible, and dfs_query_then_fetch is needed to fix the problem. This performs an initial round trip to all shards and retrieves the index statistics, and then the coordinating node will send the merging statistics to the shards alongside the request.

How to tune for indexing speed

Now, let's understand how we can tune the indexing speed of Elasticsearch. Here, we will cover different ways to improve indexing performance; let's start with bulk requests.

Bulk requests

Bulk requests have better performance than single-indexed document requests. Users are recommended to run a benchmark on a node containing a shard, and to index 100 documents at once, slowly doubling the number. Once a plateau is observed in the indexing speed, the optimal size of the data request has been reached. It's better to avoid large bulk requests as they might put the cluster under memory pressure; a recommended size is a few megabytes per request.

Smart use of the Elasticsearch cluster

To make better use of an Elasticsearch cluster, users are recommended to use multiple threads and processes to send data. Better utilization of a cluster also leads to a reduced cost of `fsync`. The response code for `EsRejectedExecutionException` indicates `TOO_MANY_REQUESTS(429)`—meaning the indexing rate is too much for Elasticsearch to handle. This can be fixed with a short pause in the indexing process before trying again. The optimal number of workers is best determined through testing. Increase the number of workers until the I/O or CPU can handle saturation.

Increasing the refresh interval

The current `index.refresh_interval` setting is 1 second, and this forces Elasticsearch to create a new segment every second. Increasing this value allows larger segments to flush, and hence decreases the merge pressure.

Disabling refresh and replicas

To load a large amount of data at once, `index.refresh_interval` should be changed to `-1` and `index.number_of_replicas` set to `0`. This will make the indexing faster, but will temporarily put the index at risk of data loss if there are any shard losses. These parameters can be returned to their initial values once initial loading is complete.

Allocating memory to the filesystem cache

The filesystem cache needs at least half of the memory of the machine running Elasticsearch. It uses the memory to buffer I/O operations.

Using auto generated IDs

When a document is indexed and a specific index declared, Elasticsearch has to check whether there is a document with the same ID in the same shard. This is a costly operation that only grows more expensive as the index grows. It is better to use auto generated IDs so Elasticsearch can index and skip the process of checking.

Using faster hardware

Related to allocating enough memory to the filesystem cache, a hardware upgrade may prove useful. SSD drives perform better than spinning disks, and it's always a good idea to use local storage and avoid remote filesystems such as NFS or SMB.

Indexing buffer size

When a node is performing heavy indexing, it uses at most 512 MB per shard. Elasticsearch uses this setting as a shared buffer for all active shards.

How to tune for search speed

In the previous section, we covered how to improve the performance of Elasticsearch indexing. Now, we will cover how to improve the search speed of Elasticsearch. There are different ways to improve the search speed, so let's start with search performance tuning.

Allocating memory to the filesystem cache

Allocate at least half of the memory to the filesystem cache. This is necessary as Elasticsearch relies heavily on the cache to make the search faster.

Using faster hardware

As mentioned previously, an upgrade of hardware can be very useful in improving speed. SSD drives perform better than spinning disks, and local storage is better than remote filesystems such as NFS or SMB. Virtualized storage might be faster than remote systems, but it's inherently slower than local storage.

Document modeling

To make the search time as quick as possible, documents should be modeled. Joins are to be avoided, and nested and parent-child relations slow down the queries.

Searching as few fields as possible

A query slows as the number of fields it targets increases. To overcome this, it is better to copy the values into a single field at index time, and then search through the field at search time. This process can be automated with the copy-to directive of mappings. In the following example, an index contains the titles and authors of books. The query indexes both values into the same `name_and_title` field. Please refer to the following example:

```
PUT books
{
  "mappings": {
    "properties": {
      "name_and_title": {
        "type": "text"
      },
      "name": {
        "type": "text",
        "copy_to": "name_and_title"
      },
      "title": {
        "type": "text",
        "copy_to": "name_and_title"
      }
    }
  }
}
```

In the preceding query, we are copying the name and title field into the `name_and_title` field.

Pre-index data

Leveraging patterns into queries optimizes the indexed data. For example, if all documents have a `size` field and most queries have range aggregations on a list of ranges, then the process can be performed faster by pre-indexing the ranges into the index with term aggregations:

```
PUT index/_doc/1
{
  "designation": "Sports shoes",
  "size": 8
}
```

After indexing the documents, we can search them using the following query:

```
GET index/_search
{
  "aggs": {
    "size_ranges": {
      "range": {
        "field": "size",
        "ranges": [
          {
            "to": 6
          },
          {
            "from": 6,
            "to": 12
          },
          {
            "from": 12
          }
        ]
      }
    }
  }
}
```

Using a keyword, the document can be furnished with `size_range` at index time:

```
PUT index
{
  "mappings": {
    "properties": {
      "size_range": {
        "type": "keyword"
      }
    }
  }
```

```
    }
  }
```

The following expression shows the indexing of a document with `size_range`:

```
PUT index/_doc/1
{
  "designation": "Sports shoes",
  "size": 8,
  "size_range": "6-12"
}
```

The search request will aggregate the new field:

```
GET index/_search
{
  "aggs": {
    "size_ranges": {
      "terms": {
        "field": "size_range"
      }
    }
  }
}
```

Using the preceding query, we can aggregate the results using the `size_range` field values.

Mapping identifiers as keywords

Elasticsearch indexes numbers as a way to optimize the `range` queries, and keyword fields optimize the `term` queries. This means that if data is sometimes numeric, it should not be always mapped as a numeric field. Certain fields benefit from being mapped as keywords.

Avoiding scripts

In Elasticsearch, we should avoid scripts for data searches as this increases the query time. But if it is absolutely necessary, then we should use the `painless` and `expressions` engines to perform the query.

Searching with rounded dates

A rounded date provides a better query cache. So, instead of matching the exact date and time, we can round the date to minutes so that we can match the date irrespective of the **seconds** part of the date. However, this might make the query a bit slower, but this caching will improve overall performance.

Force-merging read-only indices

Read-only indices will benefit from being merged into a single segment. This is the default scenario for time-based indices in which the write operation is performed on the index with the current time frame, while other indices are converted into read-only.

 Note: Do not merge indices that are still being written to.

Prepping global ordinals

Global ordinals are used to run `terms` aggregations on the `keyword` fields. To set up Elasticsearch to load global ordinals at refresh time, we should use the following code to configure mapping:

```
PUT index_name
{
   "mappings": {
     "properties": {
       "field": {
         "type": "keyword",
         "eager_global_ordinals": true
       }
     }
   }
}
```

Prepping the filesystem cache

On a restarted machine, the filesystem cache is empty and Elasticsearch will take a while to load the hot regions of the index into memory. Once done, this leads to faster operation. However, loading too many indices or too many files can slow down the search.

Using index sorting for conjunctions

Index sorting makes conjunctions faster at the cost of slower indexing. It helps to organize Lucene document IDs, which makes the search more efficient.

Using preferences to optimize cache utilization

Besides the filesystem cache, other caches affect the search performance—such as the request cache or the query cache. All of these caches are maintained at the node level.

Balancing replicas

Replicas can help to improve throughput and resiliency, but a setup with a fewer number of shards per node will perform better. Note, however, that a setup without any replicas is at risk of data loss.

How to tune search queries with the Profile API

The Profile API can be used to analyze the cost of each component of a query and aggregations. Tuning the queries to be less expensive results in better performance and reduced load. However, there are downsides to the Profile API:

- When used as a debugging tool, it can lead to additional overhead and very verbose output.
- Due to the additional overhead, the resulting took times are not reliable, as the actual took time may experience timing differences.

While it can be used to explore the reasons behind expensive clauses, the Profile API is not intended to be used for accurate measuring of the absolute timings of each individual clause.

Faster phrase queries

A text field has the `index_phrases` parameter, which allows the indexing of two shingles. It is automatically leveraged by query parsers to speed up the queries.

Faster prefix queries

A text field has the `index_prefixes` parameter that allows the indexing of prefixes of all terms. It is automatically leveraged by query parsers to speed up the queries.

How to tune for disk usage

Now, let's understand how we can tune disk usage to improve Elasticsearch performance.

Disabling unused features

Elasticsearch indexes and adds doc values by default to most fields to be searchable and aggregated out of the box. For example, the `foo` numeric field needs to be used for histograms, but it does not need a filter. So, to disable indexing on this field in the mapping, use the following query:

```
PUT index
{
  "mappings": {
    "properties": {
      "foo": {
        "type": "integer",
        "index": false
      }
    }
  }
}
```

The `text` fields store normalization factors to be able to score documents. To match capabilities on a `text` field, Elasticsearch can be configured to not write norms to the index:

```
PUT index
{
  "mappings": {
    "properties": {
      "foo": {
        "type": "text",
        "norms": false
      }
    }
  }
}
```

To determine the frequency of the word `foo`, add `"index_options": "freqs"` in the `"foo"` brackets.

Do not use default dynamic string mappings

Using default dynamic string mappings will index the string field as `text` and `keyword`. This is unnecessary, since `ID` is typically indexed as `keyword`, and a `body` field only needs to be indexed as a `text` field.

Monitoring shard size

Large shards are more efficient in storing data. To increase the size of shards, decrease the number of primary shards by creating indices with fewer primary shards, create fewer indices, or modify the existing index using the Shrink API.

Disabling source

The original JSON body is stored in the `_source` field. It is recommended to disable this field if it is not used or needed by APIs. We can disable the source using the following expression:

```
PUT index_name
{
   "mappings": {
     "_source": {
        "enabled": false
     }
   }
}
```

Using the preceding expression, we can disable the source on any index. Disabling the source has consequences, including the fact that it disables the use of the `_reindex` API.

Using compression

The `_source` and stored fields can take up a small amount of space. They can be compressed using `best_compression`.

Force merge

`_forcemerge` reduces the number of segments per shard. It can be set up to one per shard using `max_num_segments=1`. We should apply force merge to read-only indices only. To convert any index into a read-only index, we need to execute the following expression:

```
PUT index/_settings
{
  "index": {
    "blocks.read_only": true
  }
}
```

We can apply force merge to any index using `_forcemerge`; refer to the following expression:

```
POST /test/_forcemerge
```

In the preceding expression, we are applying the force merge to the test index.

Shrink indices

The Shrink API reduces the number of shards in an index. Combined with `_forcemerge`, it can significantly reduce the number of shards and segments in an index. We can use the following expression to shrink an index:

```
POST source_index/_shrink/target_index
```

Using the preceding expression, we can shrink an index; again, this can only be applied to a read-only index.

Using the smallest numeric type needed

The type of numeric data can affect disk usage. Integers should be stored as integer types, and floating points should be stored as `scaled_float`, or as the smallest type that can fit the use: `float`, `double`, or `half_float`. This way, we can reduce disk usage.

Putting fields in order

Since documents are compressed into blocks, there is a higher possibility that it will find longer duplicate strings in the source documents if fields are always in the same order. The order of fields helps us to achieve optimized disk usage, so it is necessary to follow the same order during indexing, for all of the documents of an index.

Summary

In this chapter, we have covered the bottlenecks of Elasticsearch performance and how to improve it. We started with data sparsity and explained the reason for sparsity and how it impacts performance. After sparsity, we covered and explained different solutions to common problems. We explained stemming with examples and, after that, explained inconsistent scoring. We explained different ways to tune the indexing speed, such as bulk requests, smart use of Elasticsearch clusters, increasing refresh intervals, and disabling refresh and replicas. Then, we also covered how to tune search speed through allocating memory to the filesystem cache, faster hardware, document modeling, pre-index data, avoiding replicas, and so on. Finally, we covered how to tune search queries with the Profile API and how to tune for disk usage.

In the next chapter, we will cover how to aggregate datasets and will explain the different types of aggregations that Elasticsearch supports.

7
Aggregating Datasets

Data aggregation provides us with a way to extract the information from a huge set of data and present it in a summary form. We can group the information in various buckets to get an idea of various categories or ranges. Let's take an example of a shopping site where we have complete data regarding products and their prices. Now, if we want to categorize the products into different price ranges, then we have to apply data aggregation. In the same way, we can also apply aggregation of product categories. In this chapter, we will cover the different types of aggregations that Elasticsearch provides, such as metrics, bucket, pipeline, and matrix aggregation. In this chapter, we are going to cover the following topics:

- What is an aggregation framework?
- Advantages of aggregations
- Structure of aggregations
- Metrics aggregations
- Bucket aggregations
- Pipeline aggregations
- Matrix aggregations

What is an aggregation framework?

An aggregation framework collects analytic data from a set of documents and combines the information to build complex data summaries and statistics. There are four families of aggregations, each of which has a different role:

- **Metrics**: This family of aggregations is based on the metrics on different fields of the Elasticsearch documents.
- **Bucketing**: This is a family of aggregations that build buckets. Each individual bucket is correlated to a key and a document criterion. When executing an aggregation, the bucket criteria are evaluated on all documents. A document falls in a relevant bucket if it meets the criteria. Each aggregation process will result in a list of buckets that contain documents that belong to it.
- **Pipeline**: The pipeline family aggregates the output of other aggregations and their associated metrics.
- **Matrix**: A matrix is created by extracting values from multiple fields in documents. The matrix is then used to analyze this data. It does not support scripting.

Advantages of aggregations

A significant advantage of aggregations is that they can be nested in various ways. Associating an aggregation to a bucket leads to the aggregation being executed on the contents of the bucket. A bucketing aggregation can have a sub-aggregation that will act as a parent-child. There is no limit to the depth of aggregations, so complex routines can be created.

Structure of aggregations

The structure of an aggregation is shown in the following code block. The aggregation is defined under a name, the type of aggregation is declared, and the aggregation body follows. Additional aggregations can be defined in this same level of aggregations. Please refer to the following expression, using which we can write the aggregation queries:

```
"aggregations": {
    "<aggregation_name>": {
        "<aggregation_type>": {
            <aggregation_body >
        }
        [, "meta": {[ < meta_data_body > ]}] ?
```

```
        [, "aggregations": {[ < sub_aggregation > ]}] ?
      }
      [, "<aggregation_name_2>": {...      }] *
  }
```

In the preceding expression, we have the main aggregation block, under which we can type the name of the aggregation, its type, and then the aggregation body. We can also add the sub-aggregation along with the main aggregation.

Source values are typically extracted from a specific document field, but the source can also be values from the extracted documents, or from a defined script that generates the values. A value script is a script that has the field and script settings defined, and is evaluated on a value level, whereas normal scripts are evaluated on a document level.

The `lang` and `params` parameters can be set in scripts.
The `lang` parameter defines the scripting language, and `params` defines the dynamic parameters in the script as parameters.

Metrics aggregations

The metrics aggregation family computes metrics based on values collected from the aggregated documents. Numeric metrics aggregations are a special kind of metrics aggregations that output numeric values. `single-value numeric aggregations` are aggregations that output a single numeric metric, and `multi-value numeric metrics aggregations` return multiple metrics. This is an important distinction when the aggregations are used as a sub-aggregation within a bucket aggregation. The following are some of the main metrics aggregation types:

- Avg aggregation
- Weighted avg aggregation
- Cardinality aggregation
- Extended stats aggregation
- Max aggregation
- Min aggregation
- Scripted metric aggregation
- Stats aggregation
- Sum aggregation

Now, let's cover these aggregation types in detail.

Avg aggregation

This is a single-value metric aggregation that computes the average of numeric values. The values are extracted from the aggregated document fields or from a script. For example, let's say we want to average the price of a range of backpacks in a store:

```
POST /backpack/_search?size=0
{
  "aggs": {
    "avg_price": {
      "avg": {
        "field": "price"
      }
    }
  }
}
```

The preceding expression shows an example of the `avg` aggregation, where we are applying the `avg` aggregation to the `price` field.

Weighted avg aggregation

The `weighted_avg` aggregation computes the weighted average of numeric values that are collected from aggregated documents. The formula of a weighted average is as follows:

```
Σ(value * weight) / Σ(weight)
```

The parameters in a `weighted_avg` aggregation are as follows:

- `value`: This is the configuration that provides the values for the field or script.
- `weight`: This is the configuration that provides the weights for the field or script.

The following parameters are optional:

- `format`: This denotes the format of the numeric.
- `value_type`: This defines information about the value for pure scripts or unmapped fields.

The parameters of `value` and `weight` can also both be configured. They both take the following parameters:

- `field`: This is the field name from where values are extracted.
- `missing`: If the field is missing, this value takes its place.

In our backpack example, let's say the `price` field is anywhere from $0 to $100. The `weight` field shows the most popular backpacks in the store, and the weighted average can be computed with the preceding formula by using the following command:

```
POST /backpacks/_search
{
  "size": 0,
  "aggs": {
    "weighted_price": {
      "weighted_avg": {
        "value": {
          "field": "price"
        },
        "weight": {
          "field": "weight"
        }
      }
    }
  }
}
```

The aggregation only allows one weight to be used for the calculation. If multiple weights are encountered in a document, it will throw an exception. In the case of a missing value, the `value` field will be ignored and the aggregation will continue onto the next document. If the `weight` field is missing, it will be assumed to have a weight of 1. These options can be overridden with the missing parameter.

Cardinality aggregation

This calculates an approximate count of distinct values using a single-value metrics aggregation. Values can be retrieved from fields in a document or from a script. Continuing our example from the previous section, let's index the sales of backpacks from the store:

```
POST /sales/_search?size=0
{
  "aggs": {
    "type_count": {
      "cardinality": {
        "field": "type"
      }
    }
  }
}
```

The `precision_control` option allows the user to trade memory for accuracy by defining a count below which values are expected to be accurate. Any value above this threshold will define counts as fuzzy. Note that this threshold defaults to 3,000. To compute exact counts, users need to load values into a hash set and return the size—but this is not applicable to high cardinality sets or large values. The required memory usage and the need to communicate them per shard set utilizes too many resources.

The `cardinality` aggregation is based on the **HyperLogLog++** algorithm. It counts the hashes of the values with configurable precision, with excellent accuracy on low-cardinality sets and fixed memory usage. Note, though, the important relationship between memory usage and the configured precision. A precision of threshold m will use $m*8$ bytes. On sets that have a high cardinality, pre-computed hashes can be used to provide faster storing of the hash values in the index—then, a `cardinality` aggregation can be run on the field.

Extended stats aggregation

The `extended_stats` aggregation is an extended version of stats aggregation. It will aggregate multi-value metrics to compute stats of numeric values retrieved from aggregated documents. Check the following example:

```
GET /backpacks/_search
{
  "size": 0,
  "aggs": {
    "price_stats": {
      "extended_stats": {
        "field": "price"
      }
    }
  }
}
```

This will aggregate the price statistics over the documents. The aggregation type is `extended_stats`, and the numeric field is `price`. This will also return information about the `std_deviation_bounds` object, which is used to provide visual variance of the data. To set the standard deviation to 3, set `sigma` to the value 3:

```
GET /backpacks/_search
{
  "size": 0,
  "aggs": {
    "price_stats": {
      "extended_stats": {
```

```
        "field": "price",
        "sigma": 3
      }
    }
  }
}
```

 For the standard deviation to be applicable, it needs to be normally distributed.

Max aggregation

The max aggregation returns the maximum of the numeric values extracted from a document. In the following example, we are fetching the maximum value for the price field:

```
POST /sales/_search?size=0
{
  "aggs": {
    "max_price": {
      "max": {
        "field": "price"
      }
    }
  }
}
```

Min aggregation

The min aggregation returns the minimum of the numeric values extracted from a document. In the following example, we are fetching the minimum value for the price field:

```
POST /sales/_search?size=0
{
  "aggs": {
    "min_price": {
      "min": {
        "field": "price"
      }
    }
```

```
    }
  }
```

Percentiles aggregation

This metric aggregation computes the percentiles over numeric values. In the following example, the percentile is computed in relation to load time, where the `load_time` field is a numeric field:

```
GET latency/_search
{
  "size": 0,
  "aggs": {
    "load_time_outlier": {
      "percentiles": {
        "field": "load_time"
      }
    }
  }
}
```

The `keyed` flag set to `true` will associate a unique string key with each bucket.

Scripted metric aggregation

This metric aggregation computes scripts to return a metric output:

```
POST ledger/_search?size=0
{
  "query": {
    "match_all": {}
  },
  "aggs": {
    "profit": {
      "scripted_metric": {
        "init_script": "state.transactions = []",
        "map_script": "state.transactions.add(doc.type.value == 'sale' ?
doc.amount.value: -1 * doc.amount.value)",
        "combine_script": "double profit = 0; for (t in state.transactions)
{ profit += t } return profit",
        "reduce_script": "double profit = 0; for (a in states) { profit +=
a } return profit"
      }
    }
```

```
    }
  }
```

There are four stages of scripts:

- `init_script`: This sets the initial state and is executed before any collection of documents.
- `map_script`: This checks the value of the `type` field and is executed on every document collected.
- `combine_script`: This aggregates the state returned from every shard; it is executed on every shard after document collection is finished.
- `reduce_script`: This provides access to the variable states; this variable collects the results from `combine_script` on each shard into an array.

Stats aggregation

This multi-value metric aggregation computes the stats extracted from aggregated documents. The stats can be min, max, sum, count, or avg:

```
POST /backpacks/_search?size=0
{
  "aggs": {
    "price_stats": {
      "stats": {
        "field": "grade"
      }
    }
  }
}
```

In the preceding example, we are fetching the stats for the grade field.

Sum aggregation

This metric aggregation computes the sum of numeric values extracted from aggregated documents:

```
POST /sales/_search?size=0
{
  "query": {
    "constant_score": {
      "filter": {
```

```
        "match": {
          "type": "hat"
        }
      }
    }
  },
  "aggs": {
    "hat_prices": {
      "sum": {
        "field": "price"
      }
    }
  }
}
```

In the preceding example, we are fetching the sum of the `price` field.

Bucket aggregations

Bucket aggregations create buckets of documents. Each bucket has a criterion that determines which types of document fall into it. As opposed to metrics, they can hold sub-aggregations, known as child buckets, within a parent bucket. Let's cover some of the bucket aggregation types.

Adjacency matrix aggregation

This bucket aggregation returns a form of adjacency matrix. Each bucket represents a cell in the matrix of intersecting filters. For example, given three filters, **A**, **B** and **C**, the response will return the following:

	A	**B**	**C**
A	A	A&B	A&C
B		B	B&C
C			C

The buckets B&A, C&A, and C&B are not included as they are already in the table (as A&B, A&C, and B&C). The matrix is symmetrical, and so only half of it is necessary. A `separator` parameter allows the user to modify the separator from an ampersand to a string, or anything else. This aggregation can provide all of the requested data and creates an undirected weighted graph. When used with a child aggregation, this changes, as the dynamic network analysis becomes relevant.

Auto-interval date histogram aggregation

This type of bucket aggregation sets a target number for buckets, so the request retrieves a number of buckets equal to or less than the target number by creating them at set intervals. By default, the `buckets` field is set to `10`. A key for the interval is the timestamp returned with each bucket.

Intervals

As mentioned previously, an interval is used to retrieve a certain number of buckets automatically. The interval is selected based on the aggregated data, and the following intervals can be used:

- **Seconds**: In multiples of 1, 5, 10, and 30
- **Minutes**: In multiples of 1, 5, 10, and 30
- **Hours**: In multiples of 1, 3, and 12
- **Days**: In multiples of 1 and 7
- **Months**: In multiples of 1 and 3
- **Years**: In multiples of 1, 5, 10, 20, 50, and 100.

Note the following:

- In the scenario where the number of buckets found is higher than the requested number of buckets, only one-seventh of the buckets requested will be returned.
- The `time_zone` parameter is stored in Elasticsearch in UTC. This can be changed using the following syntax: `"time_zone": "-01:00"`.
- Scripts can be used on document and value levels.
- The `missing` parameter will ignore a document by default. This can be changed to `"missing": "2010/02/02"`.

Composite aggregation

This multi-bucket aggregation creates composite buckets from various sources. It can be used to aggregate all the buckets from multi-level aggregations, thereby creating a scroll to allow streaming through all of the buckets.

The `sources` parameter defines the sources to be used to build the composite buckets. There are three types of value sources:

- `terms`: Values extracted from a field or a script
- `histogram`: Applied to numeric values to build fixed-size intervals over the values
- `date_histogram`: Very similar to the `histogram` parameter, except the interval is specified by date

Buckets are sorted by their natural ordering, and values are sorted in ascending order of their values. In the scenario where multiple value sources are requested, the ordering takes place according to per source value. Also note the following:

- The `missing_bucket` parameter neglects the documents that do not contain a value. To include these documents, set this parameter to `true`.
- The `size` parameter defines how many composite buckets are returned. The `after` parameter returns the buckets from the next results of the `size` parameter.
- Sub-aggregations are used to compute other buckets and statistics on each composite bucket within the parent aggregation.

Date histogram aggregation

This is a multi-bucket aggregation that can only be used on date values. The interval is specified using a date/time expression. In Elasticsearch, dates are represented internally as long values. The intervals can be set up as a single time unit (1 hour, 1 day), as calendar intervals, in multiple time units (7 hours, 4 days), or as fixed-length intervals. The values can be in the following:

- milliseconds (`ms`): Fixed length, supports multiples
- seconds (`s`): Fixed length, supports multiples
- minutes (`m`): Interval of a minute, starting at 00 seconds
- hours (`h`): Interval of an hour, starting at 00 minutes and 00 seconds
- days (`d`): Interval of a day, starting at midnight (00:00:00)
- weeks (`w`): Interval of a week, starting at the day_of_week:hour:minute:second
- months (`m`): Interval of a month, starting at the day:time
- quarters (`q`): Interval of 3 months, starting at month:day:time
- years (`y`): Interval of a year, starting at month:day:time

The time zone is UTC by default, but this can be changed to any other value. The offset parameter changes the start value of buckets with a positive or negative offset. The response has a key associated with each bucket and contains the ranges of intervals. It supports document- and value-level scripts. The `missing` parameter neglects documents that do not contain a value. To include these documents, set the parameter to `true`.

Date range aggregation

This aggregation is based on ranges of date values. It takes **Date Math** expressions as values of `from` and `to`. The following example takes the range from 10 months ago to 10 months from now:

```
"ranges": [
    {"to": "now-10M/M" },
    {"from": "now-10M/M" }
]
```

The `missing` parameter neglects those documents that do not contain a value. To include these documents, set the parameter to `true`. Time zones can be modified in the `time_zone` parameter to fit according to the user's needs. The `keyed` flag set to `true` will return a string key with each bucket.

Filter/filters aggregation

This defines a single and multiple buckets for the documents. The `filter` aggregation is used to reduce the aggregation to a set of documents. The `filters` aggregation associates a filter with a bucket, in which a bucket will collect documents that meet the filter standards. The `other_bucket` parameter can be defined to add a bucket that collects all the documents that do not fit into the given filters.

Geo distance aggregation

This multi-bucket aggregation applies to the `geo_point` fields. The user defines an origin point and a set of distance range buckets. The `keyed` flag set to `true` will return a string key with each bucket.

Geohash grid aggregation

This multi-bucket aggregation applies to the `geo_point` fields. It groups points into buckets, which represent cells in a grid. This results in a sparse grid that contains only cells that have a value. A geohash is used to label every cell. High-precision geohashes represent cells that cover a small area, whereas low-precision geohashes cover a large area. Geohashes have a very specific length associated with a very specific width and height.

The following options are supported:

- `field`: Name of the field that is indexed with GeoPoints
- `precision`: Optional feature that determines the string length of geohashes; defaults to 5
- `size`: Optional feature that determines the maximum number of geohash buckets to be retrieved
- `shard_size`: Optional feature that allows more accurate counting of the top cells

Geotile grid aggregation

This multi-bucket aggregation also applies to `geo_point` fields. It groups points into buckets, which represent cells in a grid. This results in a sparse grid and contains only cells that have a value. Each cell associates to a map tile. High-precision keys have a larger range for x and y and cover a small area. Low-precision keys have a smaller range of x and y and cover a large area.

The following options are supported:

- `field`: Name of the field that is indexed with GeoPoints
- `precision`: Optional feature that determines the integer zoom of the key; defaults to 7
- `size`: Optional feature that determines the maximum number of geohash buckets to be retrieved; defaults to 10,000
- `shard_size`: Optional feature that allows more accurate counting of the top cells

Histogram aggregation

This multi-bucket aggregation applies to numeric values from documents. The aggregation dynamically builds a fixed-size interval of buckets over the values. The interval must be defined as a positive decimal, and the offset is also a decimal: [0, interval).

A minimum document count will fill the gaps in a histogram with empty buckets. It can be changed using the min_doc_count setting. The buckets are returned in ascending order. They start at 0 and continue in terms of intervals. The missing parameter neglects the documents that do not contain a value. To include these documents, set the parameter to a value, "missing":0.

Significant terms aggregation

This special type of aggregation returns very specific information that occurs in a set. For example, a significant term in a book about **bird flu** might be set as **H5N1**. It returns interesting or rare terms as computed between a foreground and background set of documents.

Significant text aggregation

Similar to the significant terms aggregation, this returns information based on texts and not terms. For example, it suggests **H5N1** when the users look for **bird flu** in a text to expand queries. So this is again one step ahead of what significant terms aggregation is doing. So when a user provides the search text, the other significant terms are computed between foreground and background set of documents and displayed to the user.

Terms aggregation

This multi-bucket aggregation builds buckets dynamically; for example:

```
GET /_search
{
  "aggs": {
    "genres": {
      "terms": {
        "field": "genre"
      }
    }
  }
}
```

This will search movies according to genre.

Pipeline aggregations

Pipeline aggregations return outputs from other aggregations, and add information to the output tree. There are two families of aggregation:

- **Parent aggregations**: Pipeline aggregations that take the output from the parent aggregation and compute new buckets or aggregations to add to the existing buckets
- **Sibling aggregations**: Pipeline aggregations that take the output from a sibling aggregation and compute new buckets or aggregations to add to the existing buckets

The pipeline aggregations use `buckets_path` to reference the aggregations. This allows the pipelines to be chained. The syntax for the path is as follows:

```
PATH = <AGG_NAME>[<AGG_SEPARATOR>,<AGG_NAME>]*[<METRIC_SEPARATOR>,
<METRIC>];
```

Here, the parameters are as follows:

- `AGG_NAME`: Represents the name of the aggregation
- `AGG_SEPARATOR`: Represents the separator of the aggregation `'>'`
- `METRIC_SEPARATOR`: Represents the separator of the aggregation `'.'`
- `METRIC`: Represents the name of the metric

So now, let's cover different types of pipeline aggregations.

Avg bucket aggregation

This sibling-type aggregation calculates the average value of a metric in a sibling aggregation. The sibling aggregation must be a multi-bucket aggregation, and the metric must be numeric. It has the following syntax:

```
{
  "avg_bucket": {
     "buckets_path": "the_sum"
  }
}
```

And it takes the following parameters:

- `buckets_path`: The path to the buckets that are to be averaged
- `gap_policy`: The policy to be taken when there are gaps in the database
- `format`: The type of format the output value will have

Derivative aggregation

This is a parent pipeline that calculates the derivative of a metric in a parent `histogram` aggregation. The metric has to be numeric, while the enclosing histogram must have `min_doc_count` set to 0. It has the following syntax:

```
"derivative": {
   "buckets_path": "the_sum"
}
```

It takes the following parameters:

- `buckets_path`: The path to the buckets that are used to calculate the derivative
- `gap_policy`: The policy to be taken when there are gaps in the database
- `format`: The type of format the output value will have

To calculate a second order derivative, the derivative pipeline aggregation will be chained to another derivative pipeline.

Max bucket aggregation

This is a sibling type of aggregation that identifies the buckets that contain the maximum value of a specific metric from a sibling aggregation. It outputs the value and key for the buckets. The metric has to be numeric, and the sibling aggregation must be a multi-bucket aggregation. It has the following syntax:

```
{
  "max_bucket": {
    "buckets_path": "the_sum"
  }
}
```

It takes the following parameters:

- `buckets_path`: The path to the buckets that are used to find the maximum
- `gap_policy`: The policy to be taken when there are gaps in the database
- `format`: The type of format the output value will have

Min bucket aggregation

A sibling type of aggregation, this identifies the buckets that contain the minimum value of a specific metric from a sibling aggregation. It outputs the value and key for the buckets. The metric has to be numeric, and the sibling aggregation must be a multi-bucket aggregation. It has the following syntax:

```
{
  "min_bucket": {
    "buckets_path": "the_sum"
  }
}
```

It takes the following parameters:

- `buckets_path`: The path to the buckets that are used to find the minimum
- `gap_policy`: The policy to be taken when there are gaps in the database
- `format`: The type of format the output value will have

Sum bucket aggregation

This is a sibling type of aggregation that calculates the sum of the buckets that contain a specific metric from a sibling aggregation. The metric has to be numeric and the sibling aggregation must be a multi-bucket aggregation. It has the following syntax:

```
{
  "sum_bucket": {
    "buckets_path": "the_sum"
  }
}
```

It takes the following parameters:

- `buckets_path`: The path to the buckets that are used to find the sum
- `gap_policy`: The policy to be taken when there are gaps in the database
- `format`: The type of format the output value will have

Stats bucket aggregation

This is a sibling type of aggregation that calculates the variety of stats of the buckets that contain a specific metric from a sibling aggregation. The metric has to be numeric, and the sibling aggregation must be a multi-bucket aggregation. It has the following syntax:

```
{
  "stats_bucket": {
    "buckets_path": "the_sum"
  }
}
```

It takes the following parameters:

- `buckets_path`: The path to the buckets that are used to find the stats
- `gap_policy`: The policy to be taken when there are gaps in the database
- `format`: The type of format the output value will have

Extended stats bucket aggregation

This is another sibling type of aggregation that calculates the variety of stats of the buckets that contain a specific metric from a sibling aggregation. The metric has to be numeric and the sibling aggregation must be a multi-bucket aggregation. It provides a few more specifics than the `stats_bucket` aggregation, and has the following syntax:

```
{
  "extended_stats_bucket": {
    "buckets_path": "the_sum"
  }
}
```

It takes the following parameters:

- `buckets_path`: The path to the buckets that are used to find the stats
- `gap_policy`: The policy to be taken when there are gaps in the database
- `format`: The type of format the output value will have

Percentiles bucket aggregation

This is a sibling type of aggregation that calculates the percentile of the buckets that contain a specific metric from a sibling aggregation. The metric has to be numeric, and the sibling aggregation must be a multi-bucket aggregation. It has the following syntax:

```
{
  "percentiles_bucket": {
    "buckets_path": "the_sum"
  }
}
```

It takes the following parameters:

- `buckets_path`: The path to the buckets that are used to find the percentiles
- `gap_policy`: The policy to be taken when there are gaps in the database
- `format`: The type of format the output value will have
- `percents`: The percentiles to be calculated
- `keyed`: Returns the range as a hash

Moving function aggregation

This aggregation slides a window across data. It allows the user to specify a custom script to be executed on each window. It has the following syntax:

```
{
  "moving_fn": {
    "buckets_path": "the_sum",
    "window": 10,
    "script": "MovingFunctions.min(values)"
  }
}
```

It takes the following parameters:

- `buckets_path`: The path to the buckets that are used in the pre-built function
- `window`: The size of the window that will slide across the histogram
- `script`: The script to be executed on each window

This script takes pre-built functions, such as the following:

- `max()`: This function returns the maximum value from a window.
- `min()`: This function returns the minimum value from a window.
- `sum()`: This function returns the sum of the values of a window.
- `stdDev()`: This function returns the standard deviation of values in a window.
- `unweightedAvg()`: This function returns the sum of all the values in a window and divides by the size of it.
- `linearWeightedAvg()`: This function assigns a linear weight to the points in a series, such that the first points contribute in a less linear manner to the total average.
- `ewma()`: This function assigns an exponential weight to the points in a series such that the first points contribute exponentially less to the total average; known as a single exponential.
- `holt()`: This function assigns a second exponential term to track the data trend. It calculates two values: a **level** and a **trend**; this is known as a double exponential.
- `holtWinters()`: This function assigns a third exponential to track the seasonal aspect of the data. It calculates three values: a **level**, a **trend**, and a **seasonality**; also known as a triple exponential.

Cumulative sum aggregation

This is a parent pipeline type aggregation that calculates the cumulative sum in a parent `histogram` aggregation. It has the following syntax:

```
{
  "cumulative_sum": {
    "buckets_path": "the_sum",
  }
}
```

It takes the following parameters:

- `buckets_path`: The path to the buckets that are used to find the cumulative sum
- `format`: The type of format the output value will have

Bucket script aggregation

This is a parent pipeline type aggregation that executes a script. The script can be performed on each bucket, on specified metrics in the parent multi-bucket aggregation. It has the following syntax:

```
{
  "bucket_script": {
    "buckets_path": {
    "my_var1": "the_sum",
    "my_var2": "the_value_count"
  },
  "script": "params.my_var1 / params.my_var2"
  }
}
```

It takes the following parameters:

- `script`: The script to be run on the aggregation
- `buckets_path`: The map of script variables and the associated bucket paths
- `gap_policy`: The policy to be taken when there are gaps in the database
- `format`: The type of format the output value will have

Bucket selector aggregation

This parent pipeline aggregation executes a script that decides whether a bucket will stay in the parent multi-bucket aggregation. It has the following syntax:

```
{
    "bucket_selector": {
      "buckets_path": {
      "my_var1": "the_sum",
      "my_var2": "the_value_count"
    },
    "script": "params.my_var1 / params.my_var2"
    }
}
```

It takes the following parameters:

- `script`: The script to be run on the aggregation
- `buckets_path`: The map of script variables and the associated bucket paths
- `gap_policy`: The policy to be taken when there are gaps in the database

Bucket sort aggregation

This is a parent pipeline aggregation that sorts buckets in a parent multi-bucket aggregation. For multiple sorts, an order can be specified. It has the following syntax:

```
{
    "bucket_sort": {
      "sort": [
      {"sort_field_1": {"order": "asc"}},
      {"sort_field_2": {"order": "desc"}},
      "sort_field_3"
      ],
    "from":1
    "size":3
    }
}
```

And it takes the following parameters:

- `sort`: The field list to be sorted
- `from`: The location of the first bucket to be used; all previous ones will be truncated
- `size`: The number of buckets to be returned
- `gap_policy`: The policy to be taken when there are gaps in the database

Matrix aggregations

Matrix aggregations produce a matrix result from multiple fields. They do not support scripting. Let's cover the different types of matrix aggregations.

Matrix stats

The aggregation computes the following statistics:

- `count`: The number of samples per field
- `mean`: The average value for each field
- `variance`: The deviation of the samples from the mean per field
- `skewness`: The measurement quantifying the asymmetric distribution per field
- `kurtosis`: The measurement quantifying the shape of distribution per field
- `covariance`: The matrix that describes how changes in fields are associated with one another
- `correlation`: The covariance matrix from -1 to 1; describes the relationship between field distributions

It uses the following parameters:

- `avg`: The average of the values
- `min`: The lowest value
- `max`: The highest value
- `sum`: The sum of all values
- `median`: The median of all values

The `missing` parameter neglects those documents that do not contain a value. To include these documents, set the parameter to a specific value.

Summary

In this chapter, we have learned about Elasticsearch aggregation, by means of which we can aggregate the data to get insights. We have covered the four main types of aggregations, which are metrics, bucketing, pipeline, and matrix aggregation. We have also covered different types of aggregations within these four types.

In the next chapter, we will cover the best practices we can follow in order to manage the Elasticsearch cluster.

8
Best Practices

Elasticsearch is widely used, but that doesn't mean it's perfect. Elasticsearch projects can fail for any number of reasons, including Logstash node failure, the presence of too many shards, aggregations that are too deep, and even failures due to poorly mapped indices. Let's take a look at some of the most common causes of project failure, and how to avoid them. In this chapter, we will explain Elasticsearch best practices that we can apply to increase performance. Oftentimes, people install Elasticsearch and start using it with the default settings, which causes some performance issues, so it is advisable to tune Elasticsearch to get optimal output.

In this chapter, we are going to cover the following topics:

- Failure to obtain the required data
- The best cluster configuration approaches
- Using index templates to save time
- Using _msearch for e-commerce applications
- Scan and scroll for reading large datasets
- Rename indices
- Data Analytics using Elasticsearch

Failure to obtain the required data

One of the most common outcomes in Elasticsearch is a failed search—that is, the user not getting the desired result from the search. There are many reasons for this; for example, it may be due to the analyzer used for the search. The `standard` analyzer will break the search term into individual components (for example, **ecological footprint** will become **ecological** and **footprint**). The term used in the search will not be used for indexing.

Another reason for failed searches might be the incompatibility of the search term with the analyzed text. Note that some queries perform text analysis automatically. Failed searches might also occur because the `standard` analyzer is performing stop word removal on words such as **the** and **it**. Another cause could be the difference between the `match` query and query strings that process the text; a `match` query will return results while a `term` query will not return any. Many users will add wildcards to their search criteria to fix this problem, but this significantly slows the search.

Incorrectly processed text

Another common cause of failure is incorrectly processed text. This is often due to mapping. Adjusting searches to accommodate how things are stored can lead to this problem, and it's solved by indexing properly, according to how searches should be performed. So it's best to understand how text processing and mapping work in Elasticsearch from the get-go.

Gazillion shards problem

The **gazillion shards problem** isn't literal; it just refers to the problem of having too many shards. Each shard and index has a cost, even if they do not contain any documents. Issuing too many shards in an index will lead to failure, as the system will simply run out of memory. To avoid this, users are advised to create shards as infrequently as possible—for example, every week instead of every day.

Elasticsearch as a generic key-value store

If you are using Elasticsearch as a generic key-value store, mapping will grow uncontrollably. Imagine that you have a questionnaire. Letting users input any free-form answers to the questions will create index mappings for each key they input. As the mapping grows, the cost of each shard and index will enormously increase the memory cost. To solve this, make sure that the keys are fixed by restructuring the questionnaire. Nesting the documents could also be an option to avoid the mapping growing uncontrollably, as there is a default limit of 1,024 fields for an index.

Scripting and halting problem

Elasticsearch does not have a timeout for long-running scripts. This implies that scripts will never halt. This is a big problem, as long searches will eventually consume the search threads and future searches will be left in the queue. Once the queue reaches its maximum threshold, all future searches will be halted. To prevent this overload, it's best to use a test cluster to start the script and verify its running time. It's also important to note the behavior of users when they are in a queue. Some users mistake expensive, slow queries for failed ones, and try re-executing them thereby filling up the queue unnecessarily. Now let's look at how we can configure a cluster properly.

The best cluster configuration approaches

The best configuration approaches vary depending on the hardware you are using. The Elasticsearch cluster is a group of connected nodes, and its power relies on the distribution of tasks across these nodes. There are four types of node:

- Data nodes, which store and handle data
- Master nodes, which manage and configure cluster-wide actions
- Client nodes, which send requests to data or master nodes, according to the type of request
- Ingest nodes, which preprocess documents before indexing

As we saw in the previous sections, a node is automatically indexed and has a unique identifier. There are two types of cluster configuration for Elasticsearch: cloud and on-site configuration.

Cloud configuration

While Elasticsearch can be used with **Amazon Web Services (AWS)** or with **Google Cloud Platform (GCP)**, users are advised to use Elasticsearch Service on Elastic Cloud. This supports many more features than the other options, some of which come fully integrated for convenience. Some of these features are machine learning, Canvas, hot-warm and index curation, Elasticsearch SQL, and alerting.

If you would like to use an external cloud platform, the options that are supported by Elasticsearch are AWS and GCP. With both of these, it's best to select a region closest to your actual geographic location, as this will minimize network delays. Each cluster can be registered on a different platform and region.

On-site configuration

The other option is to configure on-site. The `config` directory contains three configuration files:

- The `elasticsearch.yml` file configures Elasticsearch.
- The `jvm.options` file configures Elasticsearch JVM settings.
- The `log4j2.properties` file configures Elasticsearch logging.

To change the location of the configuration directory, use the following command:

```
ES_PATH_CONF=/path/to/my/config ./bin/elasticsearch
```

To change the file paths, the following command can be used:

```
path.data: /var/lib/elasticsearch
path.logs: /var/log/elasticsearch
```

In the preceding expression, we are setting the data and logs path.

Data-ingestion patterns

As seen in previous sections, ingest nodes are an Elasticsearch node type that performs a set of actions on data. A task is represented by a processor, which is configured to form a pipeline.

Data-ingestion pipelines are crucial in providing analytics. The patterns they produce can help improve medical care, study purchase patterns, and even match people on Tinder!

Index aliases to simplify workflow

Index aliases are used to see logical indices only, and not physical indices—for example, they can be used as a part of index creation, where the alias is associated with the index. In the following example, we are creating aliases with the PUT query:

```
PUT /logs-2019-04-30
{
   "aliases": {
   "april_2019": {},
     "year_2019": {}
   },
   "settings": {
     "number_of_shards": 4,
     "number_of_replicas": 0
   }
}
```

The april_2019 and year_2019 aliases will be associated with the logs-2019-04-30 index log.

Aliases also support index templates, meaning that they will be easily accessible when handling time-based data.

Why use aliases?

We use aliases a lot when we have to work with live data, and they work well. We often use them with _reindex to experiment with different shards and mapping and searching combinations. An alias simplifies the task of updating mapping. Without them, users would need to reindex data, update the application, and then redeploy. Indices with aliases will be easy to modify. You can also set your program to categorize certain indices with certain aliases—for example, two indices named blog_v1, blog_v2 will always have the blogs alias attached to them. Aliases should almost always be used. Make sure that you have the apps reference the aliases.

Using index templates to save time

Index templates are templates that are automatically applied to new indices. These templates often include mappings and settings. This function simplifies the task of keeping track of logs. Say that you keep a monthly log. It would be quite time-consuming to include the same index every month, but using an index template would cut the job down significantly.

Another huge time-saving advantage of templates is when users combine multiple templates to create a complex index. By selecting a specific order for each template, the associated settings and mappings will be cascaded onto the new indices.

Using _msearch for e-commerce applications

_msearch stands for multi-search, which has wide applications in e-commerce. Elasticsearch can be used to improve e-commerce searches in many ways. It provides a fuzzy searching system for websites. It's also scalable, allowing Elasticsearch to run with only one node; therefore, it can organize multiple fuzzy search engines, making it multi-tenant. It provides operational stability, meaning that the search engine will continue to work even if one of the nodes fails. And all of this functionality is accessed in real time, as the indices expand.

Speed is particularly important in e-commerce. Elasticsearch allows for managing large amounts of data and provides search query retrieval in 10 ms. Since it is a scalable and distributed architecture, it can accommodate any number of servers and any volume of data.

Using the Scroll API to read large datasets

Working with large datasets is expensive for both the cluster and client. The Scroll API provides a *snapshot* of a large number of results. First, you need to initiate the scroll:

```
GET logs-2019-04-30/_search?scroll=30s
{
  "size": 1000,
  "query": {
    "match_all": {}
  },
  "sort": [
    {
      "_doc": {
        "order": "asc"
      }
    }
  ]
}
```

The preceding query will initiate a scroll that will return the first 1000 hits, where the order is not important. Using scroll=30s will delete the query if it takes more than 30 seconds to execute. Now, fetch the _scroll_id:

```
{
    "_scroll_id": "DnF1ZXJ5VGhlbkZldGNoBQAAAAAAAWOFnlWQVR3N3pxUjdLMn-
JLcUZpSDVkWWcAAAAAAAFjAAAAWPFnlWQVR3N3pxUjdLMnJLcUZpSDVkWWcAAAAAAAFkRZ5Vk
FUdzd6cVI3SzJyS3FGaUg1ZF1n",
    "took": 0,
    "timed_out": false,
    "_shards": {
        "total": 5,
        "successful": 5,
        "skipped": 0,
        "failed": 0
    },
    "hits": {
        "total": 584721,
        "max_score": null,
        "hits": [...]
    }
}
```

Using _scroll_id, you can retrieve the following chunk of documents:

```
GET _search/scroll
{
  "scroll": "30s",
  "scroll_id": "DnF1ZXJ5VGhlbkZldGNoBQAAAAAAAWOFnlWQVR3N3pxUjdLMn-
JLcUZpSDVkWWcAAAAAAAFjAAAAWPFnlWQVR3N3pxUjdLMnJLcUZpSDVkWWcAAAAAAAFkRZ5Vk
FUdzd6cVI3SzJyS3FGaUg1ZF1n"
}
```

This process can be repeated until all the documents are retrieved. This is a simplified and faster way of retrieving the required documents, as it performs the task in chunks rather than all at once.

To clear a scroll, simply delete the scroll_id value:

```
DELETE _search/scroll/DnF1ZXJ5VGhlbkZldGNoBQAAAAAAAWOFnlWQVR3N3pxUjdLMn-
JLcUZpSDVkWWcAAAAAAAFjAAAAWPFnlWQVR3N3pxUjdLMnJLcUZpSDVkWWcAAAAAAAFkRZ5Vk
FUdzd6cVI3SzJyS3FGaUg1ZF1n
```

Data backup and snapshots

It is important to back up a cluster and all the data it contains. We have already talked about replica shards in the previous section. These are not appropriate as a backup, as they do not provide any data protection. Instead, there is a specific API that snapshots and then restores data. The snapshot and restore API is a cluster backup mechanism that saves the current state of the cluster in a repository. We also use the reindex API to make temporary backups when making certain bulk document changes, such as _update_by_query and _delete_by_query. Back up all documents first with _reindex.

There are a few different ways to create a repository for backups. All of the following are supported:

- **Shared file systems**: fs file type
- **Read-only URLs**: url file type
- **S3**: s3 file type
- **HDFS**: hdfs file type
- **Azure**: azure file type
- **Google Cloud Storage**: gcs file type

The repository needs to be registered using the _snapshot endpoint before it can be used:

```
PUT _snapshot/my_repo
{
  "type": "fs",
  "settings": {
    "location": "/mnt/my_repo_folder"
  }
}
```

In the preceding example, the my_repo repository is registered as the snapshot repository. The file path needs to be accessible to all nodes in the cluster.

To take a snapshot, use the following command:

```
PUT _snapshot/my_repo/my_snapshot_1
```

In the preceding code, my_repo represents the repository name and my_snapshot_1 should be a unique snapshot name. This script will include all open indices. To specify indices, use the following command:

```
PUT _snapshot/my_repo/my_logs_snapshot_1
{
  "indices": "logs-*",
```

```
    "ignore_unavailable": true,
    "include_global_state": true
}
```

This will snapshot all the indices starting with `logs-` and will include all the global-state metadata.

Monitoring snapshot status

Use the `_status` endpoint to monitor data:

```
GET _snapshot/my_repo/my_snapshot_2/_status
```

Managing snapshots

To manage snapshots, retrieve information on the snapshots in a repository using the following:

```
GET _snapshot/my_repo/_all
```

To fetch information about a specific snapshot, specify it in the query as follows:

```
GET _snapshot/my_repo/my_snapshot_1
```

Deleting a snapshot

To delete a snapshot, use the following command:

```
DELETE _snapshot/my_repo/my_snapshot_1
```

Restoring a snapshot

To restore a snapshot, use the ID of the snapshot. This will retrieve all indices within that snapshot:

```
POST _snapshot/my_repo/my_snapshot_2/_restore
```

To retrieve specific indices in a snapshot, use the following:

```
POST _snapshot/my_repo/my_snapshot_2/_restore
{
  "indices": "logs-*",
  "ignore_unavailable": true,
  "include_global_state": false
}
```

This will retrieve all indices starting with `logs-` in `my_snapshot_2`.

Renaming indices

When restoring an index, you can replace the old version with the new version without having to completely replace the original.

In the following example, `rename_pattern` will rename the pattern to `logs-`, and will store the new indices under the name `restored-logs-$1`:

```
POST _snapshot/my_repo/my_snapshot_2/_restore
{
  "indices": "logs-*",
  "ignore_unavailable": true,
  "include_global_state": false,
  "rename_pattern": "logs-(.+)",
  "rename_replacement": "restored-logs-$1"
}
```

Restoring to another cluster

It is possible to restore a snapshot from one cluster to another. To do this, you need to register the repository in the new cluster:

```
POST _snapshot/my_repo/snap1
```

Then register the new repository using the following:

```
POST _snapshot/my_repo/snap1/_restore
```

This way, we can restore the snapshot and Elasticsearch will create all the indices that were available in the snapshot. Here, we have covered how to take snapshots and restore them.

Data Analytics using Elasticsearch

Gone are the days when logs were hidden in the log files only, and we used to fetch them whenever there was an issue in the system. We can now collect the logs from all possible sources and use them to get a complete insight over any application or system. It helps us to understand the complete system, and we can easily identify any possible issues before they occur. After integrating data from different sources we can create a centralized dashboard that can help us in any sort of decision making. This ensures that we are getting all sorts of information in front of us to help us make any decisions.

Elasticsearch, along with complete Elastic Stack, provides us with a great tool for data analytics and we can analyze any type of data. It provides us with different tools to fetch the data from different sources. For example, by using Logstash we can fetch data from RDBMS or CSV files, and system or application logs from any other external source. Elasticsearch is used to store that data and to apply data analysis through aggregation and other means, while Kibana provides us with a UI for data analysis and visualization. It also provides other options such as Machine Learning, using which we can easily find data anomalies or predict future trends. If you want to learn more about data analytics using Elastic Stack, then please refer to my book "Learning Kibana 7".

Summary

In this chapter, we have covered best practices that we can use to manage Elasticsearch clusters. We started by learning about why a project can fail and how we can avoid common mistakes. Then we covered the best cluster configuration approaches, looking at cloud configuration, on-site configuration, and so on. We also covered data backup and snapshots, among other topics. By looking at these topics, we learned about different best practices that we can follow to improve Elasticsearch cluster performance.

Other Books You May Enjoy

If you enjoyed this book, you may be interested in these other books by Packt:

Advanced Elasticsearch 7.0
Wai Tak Wong

ISBN: 978-1-78995-775-4

- Pre-process documents before indexing in ingest pipelines
- Learn how to model your data in the real world
- Get to grips with using Elasticsearch for exploratory data analysis
- Understand how to build analytics and RESTful services
- Use Kibana, Logstash, and Beats for dashboard applications
- Get up to speed with Spark and Elasticsearch for real-time analytics
- Explore the basics of Spring Data Elasticsearch, and understand how to index, search, and query in a Spring application

Elasticsearch 7.0 Cookbook - Fourth Edition
Alberto Paro

ISBN: 978-1-78995-650-4

- Create an efficient architecture with Elasticsearch
- Optimize search results by executing analytics aggregations
- Build complex queries by managing indices and documents
- Monitor the performance of your cluster and nodes
- Design advanced mapping to take full control of index steps
- Integrate Elasticsearch in Java, Scala, Python, and big data applications
- Install Kibana to monitor clusters and extend it for plugins

Leave a review - let other readers know what you think

Please share your thoughts on this book with others by leaving a review on the site that you bought it from. If you purchased the book from Amazon, please leave us an honest review on this book's Amazon page. This is vital so that other potential readers can see and use your unbiased opinion to make purchasing decisions, we can understand what our customers think about our products, and our authors can see your feedback on the title that they have worked with Packt to create. It will only take a few minutes of your time, but is valuable to other potential customers, our authors, and Packt. Thank you!

Index

Made in the USA
Coppell, TX
30 January 2021